THOMAS DOGGETT
DECEASED

FINISH OF THE RACE FOR DOGGETT'S COAT AND BADGE.
From the original by Rowlandson in the British Museum.

THOMAS DOGGETT
DECEASED

A FAMOUS COMEDIAN

PART I. THE MAN
By THEODORE ANDREA COOK

PART II. THE RACE
By GUY NICKALLS

𝕽𝖎𝖈𝖍𝖒𝖔𝖓𝖉:
TIGER OF THE STRIPE
2009

This edition first published
in 2009 by
Tiger of the Stripe
50 Albert Road
Richmond
Surrey TW10 6DP

Original edition published
in 1908 by
Archibald Constable & Co.
on behalf of the
Fishmongers' Company

ISBN 978-1-904799-50-4

Printed in the United States
& the United Kingdom by
Lightning Source

IN
PIAM
MEMORIAM

Preface to the Tiger of the Stripe Edition

T HIS book was originally published in 1908 by Archibald Constable & Co. for the Fishmonger's Company, one of the twelve great livery companies of the City of London. This was appropriate because it was to the Fishmongers that Thomas Doggett entrusted the bequest which was to pay for the annual Coat and Badge race of young watermen along the Thames.

Strangely, the present edition has been prepared as a keepsake for a quite different organisation, a society devoted not to the 'mistery' of Fishmongers but to the black art of printing and other allied trades and professions. The occasion for its publication is a Chairman's Luncheon for the members of the Committee. As I intend to sell this book to the general public and as the society has taken a doggedly non-commercial stance over the years, which has helped to maintain a great sense of happy comradeship among members, I shall not name it here.

My house being a miserable hovel on the fringes of the metropolis, I was obliged to search elsewhere for a suitable venue for the occasion and this led me, after several false starts, to Doggett's Coat and Badge public house on the South bank of the Thames. That, in turn, led me to this fascinating volume, a book far too interesting to be restricted to the members of the Committee.

Unfortunately, I only found a copy of *Thomas Doggett Deceased* about three weeks before the Luncheon. I would have liked to reset the book, add some more pictures and expand it with information on the race after 1908, some notes and an index but this is quite impossible in the time available.

The book is largely the same as the 1908 edition but the page size is slightly smaller and I have reduced the text to ninety-five percent of the original size, although some of the illustrations have been enlarged. The plates were printed as tip-ins with nothing on the reverse in the original edition and I have taken the opportunity to remove the blanks and repaginate the book. The fold-out map has been converted to a two-page spread. The frontispiece was reproduced in (rather sludgy) colour in the 1908 edition. I have increased the colour saturation and reproduced it on the cover.

The original edition had no information about the authors, so I shall devote the rest of the Preface to brief biographies.

Theodore Andrea Cook

Sir Theodore Andrea Cook (1867–1928) studied Classics at Wadham College, Oxford, where he won a Rowing Blue. After graduating, he stayed on in Oxford as a private tutor, teaching, among others, Ralph Pulitzer, son of the founder of the Pulitzer Prize. As a member of the council of the British Olympic Association, he played a major role in bringing the Games to London in 1908. Cook later became a sporting journalist on the *Daily Telegraph* before being appointed Editor-in-Chief of *The Field*. In this unlikely setting, he wrote a series of articles attacking German militarism, published in book form as *The Mark of the Beast*. He was knighted in 1916.

Guy Nickalls

Guy Nickalls (1866–1935) went to Eton where he rowed with great success, winning the Ladies' Plate in 1885. He continued his rowing at Magdalen College, Oxford. In the light of Sir Theodore Cook's comment (p. xii) on the forthcoming 1908 Olympic Games, it is particularly pleasing to note that his co-author won a gold medal in them, rowing in a Leander eight at the age of nearly forty-two. He died from injuries sustained in a car crash in 1935.

P. M. D.

RICHMOND
July 2009.

Preface

THE publication of this book was authorized by the Fishmongers' Company, for whom a special edition has been
printed in addition to that issued to the public, as a record of what
is known of Thomas Doggett, the famous Comedian, deceased,
and of the Wager which he endowed to commemorate the accession
of George I in 1714. For the pages referring to the sculling-race
Mr. Guy Nickalls, formerly amateur champion of the Thames,
is responsible. The biography of Thomas Doggett has been
written by myself, and is a much enlarged and amended version
of a short life I published some years ago in the *Monthly Review*,
all the remaining copies of which are in the possession of the
Fishmongers' Company.

The thanks of the authors are due, and are hereby very
heartily given, to Mr. J. Wrench Towse, Clerk of the Fishmongers'
Company, and Mr. White, Clerk of the Watermen's Company;
to Mr. A. M. Broadley, whose very valuable collection of pictures,
portraits, caricatures, manuscripts, and memoranda, indispensable
to any history of Doggett or his Wager, has been freely used; to
Mr. John T. Doggett, who secured for me a copy of the *History
of the Doggett-Daggett Family* by Mr. Samuel B. Doggett, of Boston,
Mass.; to Mr. Hugh Doggett, of Bristol, for an original holograph
letter signed by Doggett and in the handwriting of the subject of
these pages; to Mr. B. J. Angle for much useful help; to Mr.
G. H. Vize for the engraving of Broughton, the famous prize-
fighter and winner of this Wager, and for the Chelsea china figure
here reproduced made (temp. Geo. II.) at the works near the
Old Church, Chelsea, close to the finish of the course; to " Doggett
Cobb," Waterman, of Putney, for the interesting document relating

to his ancestor ; to William G. East, the King's Bargemaster, for
valuable assistance ; to the Editor of the *Sphere* for the picture of
one of the old races; and to several others whose kindly help
and interest have not been less appreciated because they are not
more clearly specified.

The only authentic portrait of our hero, Thomas Doggett,
which we can discover to exist is the engraving of the actor dancing
the Cheshire Round, published in George Daniel's *Merrie England*,
after an eighteenth century painting formerly preserved at the
Duke's Head, Lynne Regis, Norfolk. There is also a small portrait in colours in Mr. Broadley's extra-illustrated volumes on
the History of *Richardson's Show*. This seems to me to be another
version of the Norfolk original, to which Tory Aston evidently
refers in the passage : " Whoever would see him pictured may
view him in the character of Sawney at the *Duke's Head*, in Lynne
Regis, Norfolk." Nothing can be certainly advanced as to the
authenticity of the painting in the Garrick Club to which the
name of Doggett has been attached apparently on the authority
of the catalogue of the sale at which it was last purchased.

The name " Doggett " has been so spelt in these pages because it is thus given in Doggett's own handwriting both in the
signature of his will, and in an original letter here reproduced.

The illustrations, which will, it is believed, throw a valuable
light on many points hitherto in dispute, have been chosen with
great care from the material available. Fortunately for us the
Race inspired Rowlandson in two of his most delightful water-
colour drawings of river life. The original, representing the
finish in Chelsea Reach, is in the British Museum, and is reproduced here from the blocks (which Mr. John Murray kindly
allowed me to purchase) made for the *Monthly Review* article.
The other original is in my own possession.

It may be noted that an engraving published in 1853 shows
that the famous badge exhibited the word " Liberty " on a
scroll above the " wild horse of Hanover," with the words " The
Gift of Thomas Doggett, the late Comedian," on another scroll
beneath, and the date 1853. This is different from the badge

used in 1907 and reproduced on the cover of this book; and the original orange colour of the coat has also been changed to red.

It was pleasant to find, in the course of our researches, that advice was forthcoming from so sympathetic a predecessor as Charles Lamb, who wrote to William Hone on July 25, 1826, telling him that "the fourth of August is coming. Doggett's coat and badge, a day on the water. You will find a good deal about him in Cibber's *Apology*, octavo, facing the window, and something haply in a thin blackish quarto among the plays facing the fireside." I hope that of such hints I have duly taken advantage, but I can find no confirmation in any credible authority of the suggestion made by one writer, that Doggett was a frequent visitor to the Stock Exchange in his later years. Neither his cautious personality nor the facts of his previous career make it probable that the evening of his life was spent in speculation.

The Sporting Press of the eighteenth century, in which Mr. Nickalls was condemned to search for most of his information about the list of winners (which he has made far more complete than it ever was before) was neither so copious nor so accurate as its modern representative. But it has its consolations. The folowing statement (in 1782) is, for instance, one of the most extraordinary results of physical fatigue—if I read it aright—that has ever been recorded.

"These two kept pretty nearly abreast of each other," says the scribe, "till they came pretty nigh the goal, when the first man's skull split, which retarded him so much that the second man got in first."

It is a curious coincidence that while these pages were passing through the press I read, in the Programme of the Chelsea Pageant, which will be over before the public sees them, an Episode in which Doggett promises, in Don Saltero's tavern (close to my study windows), to give a prize for Thames Watermen in commemoration of the accession of the Hanoverian House, and adjourns to the *Swan Inn* on Chelsea Embankment (as it is called now) to inaugurate his Race for the Coat and Badge in very distinguished company, including Swift, Addison, Gay, Steele, Pope

and Handel.   The presence of the last-named celebrity is explained
by the following sentence which I quote from the Programme of
the Chelsea Pageant : " The Episode is followed by a brief tableau
representing a regatta held in the following year (1715), when
the Coat and Badge was first competed for *under the eyes of George I*.
It was for this occasion that Handel composed, and it was opposite
the *Swan Inn* that he first performed the celebrated " Water
Music."   Fortunately I find, in previous pages of the Programme
quoted, that for the purposes of the Chelsea Pageant " it has
been thought desirable to treat a local legend which is of general
acceptance as a historical fact."   I can find no other basis for
the presence of George I at the race of 1715, if race there was ;
and I must leave it to the Musicians to say whether Handel was
indeed inspired by Doggett's Wager.   The reasons   for and
against the occurrence of a race before 1716 are stated on page 51.

I feel that the year in which the Olympic Games are being
celebrated in London will not be inappropriate for the appearance
of this little history of a sporting wager which can boast the longest
continuous existence of any event of the kind in the world.   That
the race should have attained this unique position is almost entirely
due to the City Company, which has done so much, for nearly
two hundred years, to preserve the sportsmanship and dignity
of Doggett's Coat and Badge ; and I am glad to take an opportunity of acknowledging, by the tribute of these unpretentious
pages, my sense of the honourable privileges conferred by member-
ship of the ancient Mistery of Fishmongers.

T. A. C.

CHELSEA,
    July, 1908.

Contents

Part I. The Man
By Theodore Andrea Cook

Part II. The Race
By Guy Nickalls

APPENDICES

List of Illustrations

Part I

THE MAN

BY THEODORE ANDREA COOK

A Waterman, in Chelsea China.

CHAPTER I

The Fame of Actors

Where are the passions they essayed,
　And where the tears they made to flow ?
Where the wild humours they portrayed
　For laughing worlds to see and know ?
Othello's wrath and Juliet's woe ?
　Sir Peter's whims and Timon's gall ?
And Millamant and Romeo ?
　Into the night go one and all.

IT is probable that of the few who will recognize the name of Thomas Doggett in any connexion, by far the greater number will only recall the famous Race for his Coat and Badge which takes place every August " for ever " from London Bridge to Chelsea. No stranger proof could be adduced of the thin thread by which an actor's reputation hangs. It is as if the boys of 1990 should remember the name of Charles Wyndham only by a surviving challenge-cup for athletic sports which may well be among his many unknown generosities. Some such penalty is laid upon all artists who depend for their success upon a momentary appeal to an audience that is never the same. I have long ceased to wonder that a great singer should demand a thousand pounds a night, or that a successful actor should multiply his gains by skilful management. Their reward is with them, and their day is soon over.

Few, indeed, in any century, are the actors picked out for immortality by such a burial-place as that in which the body of Sir Henry Irving was so lately laid beside that of David Garrick. We sometimes think that the actor has only in this last generation come into his kingdom ; but Garrick's pall-bearers in 1779 were the Duke of Devonshire, Lords Camden, Ossory, Spencer, Pal-

merston and Sir Watkin Wynne, and among the mourners near
Shakespeare's monument, on that February day in Westminster
Abbey, were Burke, Fox and Dr. Johnson. Garrick and Irving
are the only two actors who, by their personality as much as by
their eminence in their profession, earned a grave within the
Abbey walls. But many other famous heroes and heroines of
the footlights have been commemorated there, or lie buried in
the cloisters. Under both these categories are several friends
of Thomas Doggett.

Booth, for instance (1681–1733), whose brilliant performance
in Addison's *Cato* led to a partnership that directly produced
Doggett's rupture with his associates, has in the Abbey a memorial
erected by his wife, Hester Santlow, the famous dancer. At the
south end of the cloisters lies the body of Thomas Betterton
(1635–1710), whom Doggett knew in Dorset Gardens, in Drury
Lane, and the Haymarket. It is a good instance of dramatic
tradition, by the way, that Betterton is recorded to have been
taught the part of Hamlet by Davenant, who told him how Taylor
had been instructed to act it at the Blackfriars Theatre by Shakespeare himself. In the east cloister of the Abbey is another of
Doggett's friends, the beautiful Anne Bracegirdle, with whom
he acted in several of Congreve's best comedies. At the west
end of the nave, beneath the monument to Congreve, was buried
her great rival, Nance Oldfield (1683–1730), who lay in state in
the Jerusalem Chamber.

A compatriot of Doggett's, Spranger Barry, lies in the cloisters
beside his wife, as celebrated in her time (1734–1801) as he; and
near by is the grave of Colley Cibber's daughter-in-law, who
acted with Garrick at Drury Lane until her death. Hannah
Pritchard is another of the famous band of Garrick's actresses
who are commemorated in the Abbey, and it will be remembered
that her " Lady Macbeth " earned the warm commendation of
the fastidious Horace Walpole. Greatest of all that vanished
company of the fair, Mrs. Siddons has her statue in the St. An-
drew's chapel near that of her brother, John Philip Kemble.

David Garrick, Sarah Siddons, Henry Irving—of them all

lying there, commemorated yet not remembered in the Abbey—
these three alone still keep a real and constant hold upon the
public heart ; and even of this mighty trio it is not so much their
special genius as their personality that counts for most with us
now. We would far rather read to-day of the bets which Garrick made with Charles James Fox than study his interpretation
of the most famous of his rôles. It is not the Abbey that has
given even these their immortality. So we must not think Thomas
Doggett lost so very much, after all, when he failed to win the
special form of posthumous distinction awarded to so many of
his comrades. It would indeed be difficult to select any single
artist in the first rank of his profession who was ever so utterly
forgotten for his own art, and so keenly and constantly remembered by those of an entirely different occupation, as the " famous
comedian, deceased," who founded the Race for Doggett's Coat
and Badge. It is grotesque ; but I can confidently assert that
the recurrence of the rowing season has for nearly two hundred
years drawn to the actor the attention of more people than ever
applauded or ever knew anything about his efforts on the stage.
The reason for this goes back at least as far as August 1, 1716.

Early that morning all the Thames-side watermen and their
apprentices were discussing with the greatest interest a placard
which had been set up on London Bridge the night before. It
ran as follows :—

THIS BEING THE DAY OF HIS MAJESTY'S HAPPY ACCESSION TO THE THRONE
THERE WILL BE GIVEN BY MR. DOGGETT AN ORANGE COLOUR LIVERY WITH
A BADGE REPRESENTING LIBERTY TO BE ROWED FOR BY SIX WATERMEN THAT
ARE OUT OF THEIR TIME WITHIN THE YEAR PAST. THEY ARE TO ROW FROM
LONDON BRIDGE TO CHELSEA. IT WILL BE CONTINUED ANNUALLY ON THE
SAME DAY FOR EVER.

Those who had attended the last performance at Drury Lane
were aware, from an announcement in the play-bill, that if they
desired to see the start they would have to be in the parlour of
the Old Swan Inn before four o'clock. The hour now varies
with the tide, and the falling of August 1 on a Sunday makes a
slight change in the date. But the race has taken place ever

since, and it is older than the oldest regular aquatic contest by over a century, and more ancient than any annual sporting event by sixty years; for the University Boat Race began in 1829, and the St. Leger (which antedates both the Derby and the Oaks was only instituted in 1776.

Proverbial facts are among those which are most easily forgotten, so I may remind my readers that Queen Anne died on August 1 exactly two years before Mr. Doggett's announcement caused so much stir from Rotherhithe to Richmond. Our friend was "a Whig up to the head and ears," and it is easy to imagine him making his congee with the rest of the crowd some six weeks afterwards, when Marlborough was welcoming George Louis, Elector of Hanover, to the throne of George I of England; but his moral backbone was of the stiffest, as we shall find, and I suspect he was more inclined to gloat over the defeat of Swift and all his friends than to join good-natured Dicky Steele in recommending rebels to mercy.

By that date Doggett had retired from the stage and sold out of his partnership with Wilks and Cibber in Drury Lane. He only played once more, and that was to give his adored Hanoverian sovereign the gratification of admiring his most loyal subject in his famous characters of " Ben " and of " Hob," a rôle which had earned the special commendation of Steele in the *Spectator*. His career upon the boards had been strenuous and varied, since as an unknown Irishman he had travelled from Dublin to try his luck as "leading comic" across the water. He scarcely saw Castle Street again, for his venture proved sufficiently successful to afford a somewhat striking example of that union between Celtic wit and Saxon business qualities which must be difficult for any actor to preserve, and rare for any Irishman to possess.

There are, indeed, many traits in his character which lead me to imagine that had he not found the stage an easier way to moderate fortune than another he would not have remained an actor. He objected, for instance, very strongly when Wilks once gave a benefit at Drury Lane to two entirely unknown actors from Dublin, apparently forgetting altogether that he owed his

COLLEY CIBBER,
From the engraving by Hopwood.

own advancement to similar consideration for a stranger. It took all Colley Cibber's art to smooth down his anger at such unbusinesslike proceedings, and poor Wilks had actually to pay out of his own pocket the ten pounds loss on the night (which Doggett had shrewdly foreseen) in order to keep the peace.

This is as much as to say that the respectable money-making side of our hero was more prominent than might perhaps have been desirable; and I fear I cannot claim that Doggett was a genius; but he was painstaking, industrious and trustworthy, and he earned the frequent admiration of both Addison and Steele. An actor who could please critics of an equivalent calibre to-day would be fully deserving of as well expressed a praise; and it is, to my mind, a very open question whether our loss in one direction has been made up for by our gain in the other.

It may be as well to remember the businesslike and militant side of his personality before describing his career in greater detail, in order that facts may be understood in their true light which might otherwise appear distorted. A good example of the conscientiousness which accompanied it is to be found in the great reputation he always possessed for a clever "make-up." " I can only copy Nature," Sir Godfrey Kneller told him once, " from the originals before me; while you vary them at pleasure and yet preserve the likeness." The painter has his revenge, for whatever modern art may say of his " Van Dyck and Water " at Hampton Court, his canvases remain to this day, and are but mellowed by the touch of Time; while Doggett has gone "into the night," and vanished into as dead a silence as the laughter of his merry audiences.

It may be interesting, too, to give some idea at once of the prizes of " the profession " in those days. There are many sources of evidence, but I will choose one with which the Irish actor was connected. One night after acting *Cato* Booth was given fifty guineas which had been collected in the boxes; and Doggett, with a skilful eye to the value of an advertisement that was as characteristic as his usual thriftiness, at once proposed that his own managers should make a similar presentation, " to recommend their liberal spirit—the skill of the best actor never having received such a reward in one day before." Doggett recognized that Booth had made a real hit; and he was evidently right, for Pope, imitating Horace, quotes the same celebrated part as an example his readers would recognize at once :—

> Booth enters! Hark the universal peal!
> But has he spoken? Not a syllable—
> What shook the stage and made the people stare?
> Cato's long wig, flower'd gown, and lacker'd chair.

That the business which Doggett helped to organize and conduct did credit to his capacity for management may be argued from the fact reported by Colley Cibber that the actors never took a written agreement when they were engaged, considering that the daily pay-roll was ample security, and being well aware that all outstanding demands were scrupulously satisfied before the managers took a single penny for themselves each Monday morning. This was a trifle over-confiding on the part of the actors, inasmuch as Doggett's little company of acting-managers was in so strong a position that they could have secured a new star to fill a vacancy with far greater ease than any "Hamlet" out of work could have discovered so good a management ready and able to engage him. Again, perhaps, an evidence of "business capacity." But I will not labour the point; and I return with greater pleasure to the early struggles of our Irishman before success had taught him how to save.

CHAPTER II

Bartholomew Fair

Frontem nugis solvere disce meis.

IT has been stated, in volumes which are usually considered to be authoritative, that Doggett made his first appearance upon the English stage at Bartholomew Fair. This may be perfectly possible, but the details given in an unguarded moment by the aforesaid authority are sufficient to prove that whenever Doggett really visited that ancient place of revelry it was not "at Parker and Doggett's Booth near Hosier End," nor in the play of *Friar Bacon or the Country Justice* that he made his earliest bow to English audiences. For he was certainly acting at Drury Lane in 1691, which was probably the result of several previous and unrecorded efforts ; and of his booth with Parker at Hosier Lane there is no mention in the annals of the Fair before that date, and there is a distinct mention of it in 1702.

More than this. The play about Friar Bacon is specifically named by Edward Ward in the year 1699 in his *London Spy*, Parts 9 and 10. This busy chronicler reports that he found by a visit to Drury Lane that "all the wiser part of the family of Tom Fools had translated themselves to Bartholomew Fair, tempted by the fifteen or twenty shillings a day there to be earned." From what we know of Doggett already, he was not likely to miss a good chance of turning an honest penny when the hot August weather drove so many of his audience from the pit of the theatre to the booths at Smithfield. So there "The Spy" finds him manfully running "the hazard of losing that reputation in the Fair which he'd got in the Playhouse." From what has just been said, it is evident that some mistake has arisen as to our hero's first appearance, owing to a confusion of the various accounts I have quoted. But there is no reason whatever to deny the possibility of his having tried his 'prentice hand on his first English audience under circumstances which were very favourable to utter oblivion in case of failure.

No doubt it was either in the year 1689 or 1690 that Doggett first began to be well known in London with a travelling company; and it would be an interesting coincidence if it could be shown that Doggett, the sturdy Whig of later Hanoverian days, had definitely made up his mind to renounce the Dublin stage just when James II (the Stuart king who had been declared by Parliament two months ago to have " abdicated the Government ") landed at Kinsale and entered the Irish capital in March, 1689, with Tyrconnel. If this could be proved, it would be as good an example of Doggett's wisdom as of the strength of his political convictions; for, as we know now, the Stuart cause was to be no more fortunate in Ireland than it was in Scotland during those turbulent times. By the next year James had been defeated and driven out of the country at the battle of the Boyne ; and in 1691 Tyrconnel died after the French General St. Ruth was beaten at Aughrim. By this last date Doggett was comfortably established in a good part at Drury Lane; and if my previous surmises have been correct, where we have little save hypothesis to go upon, the year of 1689 would have been a particularly auspicious moment for an Irishman to have made his bow before a London audience chiefly composed of the lower orders. The reasons for this conclusion can be briefly stated, and are not without an interest of their own.

In this same year of 1689 was acted at Bartholomew Fair " a tragi-comedy " entitled *The Royal Voyage or the Irish Expedition,* of which the first part is still extant, " printed for Richard Baldwin in the Old Bailey A.D. 1690." As literature it is not of very high importance, but its value consists in giving us a very fair example of the kind of claptraps most successful in a mixed crowd at that period. Among the dramatis personae are Tyrconnel, Nugent, Hamilton, Macarthy, Butler and others, and the author apologizes for having introduced into his play one Irishman "brave and honest (as far as his cause would let him be) to foil the rest." The sympathetic and generous reader has no doubt already anticipated my own conclusion, that in a play where native Irish humour would have been so valuable an asset, the "brave and honest" part of Macarthy may have fallen to friend Doggett. I cannot resist a short quotation before I leave the subject. "Let's o'er to England," advises the impetuous Nugent, with a rush of tempting detail :—

> That golden Land where Palms and Laurels wait us,
> Delicious Murthers and sweet Massacres :
> Hang Drown Stab Burn Broil Eat Damn our Proud Conquerors !

As an aid to rhetoric this might really be recommended to some of the Irish members. Calmer counsels, however, are urged in words that are not without their significance still :—

> The English sooner cheated are than Beaten
> We must expect a formidable Army
> Shortly in our Bowels ; though their hands
> Are raising long, they generally fall heavy.

In a later scene :—

> Enter an Irish Rabble, Men, Women, and Children, the Men with Swords and Clubs, the Women with Skenes, the Children with wooden Swords and Knives. A Piper before 'em (as was their usual Custom) with a Prey of black and small Cattle which they had robbed the English of.

Representations of the defence of Inniskillen and the siege of Londonderry follow, and the play closes with disorder in Schomberg's troops and the glorious arrival of King William at Carrickfergus, displaying "The Royal Fleet at the Bay of Bangor. The Mary Yacht with the standard. All the shore enlightened with Bonfires." When the spectators of that astonishing tableau had departed, they would probably have valued their entertainment a little more had they realized that it was the last political satire of the kind allowed at the Fair. Giantlike young men, obese ladies, grimacing Spaniards, and monsters from Antipodean fairylands were alike unequal to the task of filling up the gap, though they had done well enough for Mr. Secretary Pepys some years before. The actors were obliged to fall back upon, politically innocuous mysteries like *Susanna and the Elders*, or such plays as that in which Doggett is known to have performed in later years.

"The Spy" has many matters that are worth recording of this Bartholomew Fair, and we may as well gather up what little evidence there is of Doggett's connexion with it before following him to a more famous and remunerative stage. Driving to the hospital gate at Smithfield, "The Spy" fled from the "Belphegor's concert" of the crowd to a convenient chamber where he could fortify himself with a pipe and a draught of small ale bittered with colocynth. The air outside was thick with a compound of over-roasted pork and less polite comestibles. Clowns and posture-makers were bidding against each other for the favours of the crowd, and Matthew Prior has preserved the gist of one of their addresses in his own verse. The merry-andrew (who may very likely have been William Phillips) walked about with a neat's tongue in one hand and a black pudding in the other, and on being asked the reason he announces that he typifies a good sound rule of life :—

> *Be of your Patron's Mind whate'er he says ;*
> *Sleep very much ; think little ; and talk less ;*
> *Mind neither Good nor Bad, nor Right nor Wrong ;*
> *But eat your Pudding, slave, and hold your Tongue.*

Venturing at length out of the stronghold of his first refuge, "The Spy" tried the rope-dancing and tumbling booths, the smoky corners where pigs and pies were baking, and so, through a swarm of pedlars, mountebanks and pickpockets, to the play of Friar Bacon and Master Thomas Doggett. Among the attractions were a Royal Court, a Conjuration of the Devil, a rascal Miller, his idiot son Ralph (the very part for Thomas), a Justice Shallow, a "Flying Shoulder of Mutton," and a Ballet of Fiends. These took three-quarters of an hour to exhibit themselves, and were repeated at intervals of thirty minutes.

Alas, poor Doggett! This was in 1699. Three years later we have further evidence that our Irish friend was not afraid of rivalling the Smithfield Scaramouches, or of being seen among

the waxworks and conjuring performances of the Fair. For in
1702 the colleague of Betterton and Bracegirdle appeared at
Bartholomew's in an old woman's petticoat and a red waistcoat,
which seem more appropriate to such men as William Penkethman
(or " Pinkey," as his firm friends in the gallery called him) than
to the comedian who had made his mark at Drury Lane. However, here is the bill of his performances during the period after
the theatre had closed on August 22 in that year :—

*At Doggett's Booth at Hosier Lane End, during the Time of Bartholomew Fair
will be Presented a New Droll call'd the Distress'd Virgin or the* UNNATURAL PARENTS,
Being a true History of the FAIR MAID *of the West or the Loving Sisters, with the
Comical Travels of Poor Trusty in Search of his Master's Daughter, and his Encounter
with Three Witches. Also Variety of Comick Daunces and Songs with Scenes and
Machines never seen before. Vivat Regina.*

In 1704 this same booth was taken by Doggett and Parker,
who gave *Bateman, or the Unhappy Marriage,* while Bullock
Simpson and Norris were acting *Jepthah's Vow,* in another corner,
with the indomitable Penkethman.

This latter was a better actor than this slight reference might
perhaps indicate ; for he has earned himself a place in the *Spectator* (for May 5, 1712), where Steele says :—

Mr. Penkethman is also Master of as many Faces in the Dumbscene as can be
expected from a Man in the Circumstances of being ready to perish out of Fear and
Hunger : He wonders throughout the whole Scene very masterly without neglecting
his Victuals. If it be, as I have heard sometimes mentioned, a great Qualification
for the World to follow Business and Pleasure too, what is it in the Ingenious Mr.
Penkethman to represent a Sense of Pleasure and Pain at the same time : as you may
see him do this Evening ?

It will be seen that Doggett's example was followed by others
whose names are to be found as well in the *Spectator* as in the
playbills of Drury Lane. Nor should it be forgotten that the
Fair which had given Ben Jonson a plot for one of his comedies,
was also able to command the adaptation (for the famous Mrs.
Mynn) of a Drury Lane spectacle called *The Siege of Troy,* by
so well known an author as Elkanah Settle, the Poet Laureate,
who became a poor brother of the Charterhouse. The attractions
of Smithfield, whatever we may think of them now, were in fact

sufficient to close the doors of the few theatres in town at the end of August, and the wisest actor was no doubt he who accepted the whims of the public and continued to make money out of them all the same. Doggett was not ashamed to do so both directly and indirectly, for not only did he act in others' plays at the Fair, but a comedy of his own composing, called *The Country Wake*, was adapted to the needs of a Bartholomew's audience, before whom it was acted under the name of *Flora, or Hob in the Well*, in 1730 at Mr. Bullock's booth.

By the kindness of Mr. A. M. Broadley I am able to give a few details about Doggett's play from one of the few original copies now in existence, which is preserved in Mr. Broadley's library, and bound up with several engravings by Leguerre illustrating various scenes in what was evidently an extremely popular piece. The title-page announces "*The Country Wake*. A Comedy. As it is acted at the New Theatre in Little Lincoln's Inn Fields by His Majesty's Servants. Written by Mr. Thomas Dogget, Comedian. Printed for Sam Briscoe at the Corner of Charles Street, in Russel Street, Covent Garden; Sold by R. Wellington at the Lute in St. Paul's Churchyard; R. Parker at the Royal Exchange. Price One shilling six Pence."

DRAMATIS PERSONAE

MEN

Sir Thomas Testie	Mr. Underhill.
Woodvill	Mr. Betterton.
Friendly	Mr. Kenneston.
Old Hob	Mr. Tresise.
Young Hob	Mr. Dogget.

WOMEN

Lady Testie	Mrs. Barry.
Flora	Mrs. Bracegirdle.
Lucia	Mrs. Bowman.
Betty	Mrs. Lee.

Clowns, Servants, etc.

Scene, Glocester.

It was dedicated " to the illustrious and truly noble Prince James, Duke, Marquess and Earl of Ormond in England and

Ireland," etc., etc., in phrases which are signed by Doggett
and give us at least one curious piece of self-revelation, which
is valuable in the case of a man of whom we really know so little.
"The generality of Mankind," writes honest Thomas, who plays
the courtier with a somewhat elaborate leg, "I'm sure will think
me in the right not to prophane your Noble Character by endeavouring to describe it, which would betray my Ignorance more
than publishing this piece of Folly will do, which cost me more
time and trouble to get acted than did to Write it, except one Act
of it, which I wrote three years ago. As for its Faults, one of
them is, I hear, that it is Obscene; I'm sorry it should appear
so, I'm sure I never designed it. . . . I own there's a scarcity
of that which some call Wit, and what many Authors in this Age
run mad after, endeavouring to produce it out of everybody's
Mouth, whether it belongs to their character or no, *still losing
the Man to goe out of the way for a Jest; 'tis what I shall never
labour for, either in writing, if I were capable, or Acting; for he
that will make Nature his study will find more charms in it, and a
more certain* way to Applause than can be produced from any
abortive Conceit, which at best can but repay him with a loud
Laughter from the Multitude, who should be pleased, I own,
but not at the expence of the Author, or the Actor's reputation,
nor the Displeasure of the judicious, who I hope will not con-
demn this Play from the Appearance it had upon the Stage, when
it suffered in the Acting." The first night was, as far as I can
find, in 1696. The prologue, "spoke by Mrs. Barry," rather
exaggerated the protest of the dedication against any suspicion
of obscenity :—

> Alas ! 'tis a meer out-of-fashion Play;
> No Bawdy in't to make the Ladies glow,
> Nay, what is worse the Play's without a Beau;
> No chit-chat repartee, nor raillery. . . .

A little later, she emphasizes the double qualification of the
writer for his task :—

> The Poet would be at you, if he might,
> Did not the Player deter him from the Fight.

> He draws on your side, swears you shall not frown,
> The Comick vein shall keep the Cynick down,
> 'Twixt you and him no Quarrel yet has been ;
> If now he errs, he'll freely own his sin.

The epilogue, " spoken by Mr. Betterton," contains a most interesting simile drawn from sculling, which suggests to me that Doggett (if it be he who wrote the verses that begin and end a comedy in sturdy prose) was not unwilling to let his love of wet-bobs be known across the footlights.   The lines are as follows :—

> Writing's the fatal Rock on which has split
> Many a stout and well-built Man of Wit ;
> And yet there's not a sculler but shall dare
> To venture his week rotten Cockboat there.

Doggett, however, though ready to admit himself " less than a Dryden, Congreve, Wycherley," was not, we may imagine, very much perturbed by the possibilities of failure, and the epilogue ends in entirely his own spirit :—

> Almighty Criticks, you his Judges sit ;
> If you consent he shall set up a Wit
> He swears he won't be prouder for't a Bit.

The play is not one of those which can commend itself to every age, so I have relegated the analysis of its somewhat complicated plot (which certainly needs Mrs. Barry's " apology " for certain episodes) to the appendix.   I will only transcribe here the scene Doggett allotted to himself as Hob, a piece of writing which is near enough to the humours of the immortal Dogberry to justify any of the " almighty Criticks " in consenting that the author should be called a wit.

If the close of the love scene between Lady Testie and Woodvill shows that our author had not in vain been the friend of Congreve since 1693, this one indicates that Doggett possessed a rich fund of natural humour which many a better-known playwright of the time might have envied him.

After a conversation between Flora and Woodvill a party of rustics come on to the stage, carrying a man who has been picked up drunk in Sir Thomas Testie's orchard.   The countrymen evidently believe it is the body of some one not only a drunkard but a suicide, and the following dialogue ensues :—

Hob. Come Neighbours, bring him along, and set 'en down here, for he must be examined before we part with 'en.

Flora. How now Friends ; what Body's that you've got ?

Hob. Body—This is no Body forsooth ; this is a Carcase, one that was a wicked Body.

Flo. What has he done ?

Hob. Why he has Hanged himself.

Flo. Alas poor wretch ! What was the Cause ?

Hob. The Cause—Why he's married and has a Wife, and six Children.

Flo. Is that a Cause for a Man to hang himself ? What is he ?

Hob. What is he ? Why he's a Jacobite, and he Hanged himself because he would not pay double Taxes.

Flo. Pish—

Clown. Come Neighbour Hob, you that can tell, pray let us know what we are to do.

Hob. Why we that are the Crowner's Quest, the Law says, must enquire how he came by his Death.

Clown. But of whom must we enquire ?

Hob. Why of they that can tell, and no Body knows that so well as himself.

Clown. Well, but he's dead.

Hob. Why ay, so it seems ; and he must be buried if we say he must ; and if we say not, it may be not neither.

Clown. I suppose that's as we shall find him guilty ; therefore pray tell me, Neighbour Hob, whether you think a man that Hangs himself is guilty of his own Death or no.

Hob. Why truly that's a hard case to judge, Neighbour Clumsy.

Clown. I think now that he's guilty.

Hob. Hold, Hold, take heed, don't be too rash—for your Conscience must be Umper in this case. Look'ee, I'll put this point to you now. Whether every one that Hangs himself is willing to die ?

Clown. I—I—sure, he is willing.

Hob. Now I say No, for mayhap he might be *Non Complementus*, and if a Man be *Non Complementus* he don't know his own mind.

Clown. That's true indeed, but now being dead pray who must answer the King for the loss of his Subject ?

Hob. Marry, he that hanged his Subject : That was Himself.

Clown. Nay, Nay, 'twas the Halter that hanged him.

Hob. Aye, Aye, in some sort it did ; but that was in *Se Offendendo*, for it may be he went to break the Rope and the Rope held out in his own Defence.

Clown. But is not this same Ropemaker now, that made the Rope, in some danger ?

Hob. No, No, the Ropemaker can be in no fault ; for, d'ee see, when he makes the Rope he goes backwards and how can he see before what shall follow after ? Nor indeed is the Rope in fault, for maybe he might urge the Rope *Solus Volence*, as the Law says. Neither is he himself in fault, for maybe his

Time was come and he was born to be Hanged. Therefore I do conclude that he was conscious and guiltless of his own Death.

Clown. Why then, neighbour, he may be buried.

Hob. O, of great reason, always he that is alive must die, and he that is dead must be buried.

Clown. Yet truly I think in my Conscience he does not deserve to be buried.

Hob. O you speak partiously, neighbour Puzzlepate—not deserve to be buried, I say he deserves to be buried alive that shall Hang himself; therefore don't talk of that.

Clown. Well, but what must we do with his cloaths?

Hob. His cloaths, why they are the Hangman's.

Clown. Why then he must have 'em himself.

Hob. Hold, Hold. This is a shrewd point of Law, and must be well handled. Did he make a Will?

Clown. No, he died detestable.

Hob. Why they fall to the right Heir Male; for look 'ee d'ee see, the Female can inherit no Breeches, unless she can prove she wore them in her Husband's days.

Clown. But suppose he has no Heirs at all?

Hob. Why then they go to the Chief Mourner, and look 'ee d'ee see, that will be I, I will take his cloaths; here now I begin with his cloak—there now— let every one take a Quarter of him, and I'll follow with doleful Lamentation.

Clown. Why then we have done, Neighbour, have we?

Hob. Ay, ay.

Clown. How dolefully you look Neighbour.

Hob. Why aye; 'tis the fashion so to do; I'm Chief Mourner, I must be sad.

(*Exeunt* Omnes.)

" Hob " was naturally one of our actor's best parts. " For this reason," writes Steele in the *Spectator* (No. 502), " I have no exception to the well-drawn rusticities in the *Country-Wake*; and there is something so miraculously pleasant in Doggett's acting the aukward triumph and comick sorrow of ' Hob ' in different circumstances that I shall not be able to stay away whenever it is acted." Honest Thomas no doubt discovered that others were of the same opinion, and if Drury Lane was shut to profits, he was not fool enough to despise Hosier End. At any rate, the piece he wrote outlasted many of its time and kind; for in the form of a " Ballad-Farce," which had been given it by Colley Cibber, it was played as late as 1828.

Steele continues his criticism, which I quote from the *Spectator* for October 6, 1712 (No. 502), with a few sentences which will give some idea of his opinions of the composition, and the scene to which he refers will be found described at greater length in my appendix.

"All that vexes me," he writes, "is that Gallantry of taking the Cudgels for Gloucestershire, with Pride of Heart in tucking himself up, and taking Aim at his Adversary, as well as the other's Protestation in the Humanity of low Romance, that he could not promise the Squire to break Hob's head, but he would, if he could, do it in Love; then flourish and begin: I say what vexes me is that such excellent Touches as these, as well as the Squire's being out of all patience at Hob's Success, and venturing himself into the Croud, are Circumstances hardly taken Notice of, and the height of the Jest is only in the very Point that Heads are broken. I am confident were there a Scene written wherein Penkethman should break his leg by wrestling with Bullock and Dicky come in to set it, without one word said but what should be according to the exact Rules of Surgery in making this Extention and Binding up the Leg, the whole House should be in a Roar of Applause at the dissembled Anguish of the Patient, the help given by him who threw him down, and the handy Address and arch Looks of the Surgeon."

I need not return to Smithfield or the Fair, for it is time to mention the first appearance of our hero before a really critical and fashionable audience, nor should I have delayed thus long were it not that of Doggett almost as little has ever been published as of the vanished revelry of Bartholomew's Fair, which found its only conscientious and valuable historian in Mr. Henry Morley, almost half a century ago; to whom due greetings and farewell.

CHAPTER III

Drury Lane

Tartaream intendit vocem, qua protinus omnis
Contremuit domus . . .

THERE is, somewhat naturally, almost as much uncertainty
with regard to Doggett's first appearance as about his last;
but it is likely that he faced the public of the Theatre Royal as
" Lory " in *The Relapse*, an arch, familiar valet, whose pertness
would be especially appropriate to the Irishman's native talent.
In 1691 he was on the same boards as " Nincompoop " in
D'Urfey's *Love for Money, or the Boarding School*, and in the next
year he created " Solon " in the same author's *Marriage-Hater
Matched*, a part which seems to have confirmed his London
reputation.

But it was in 1693 that a friendship with Congreve, which
does infinite credit to the intelligence of Doggett, began to bear
fruit in a manner which must have been equally agreeable to
them both. This intimacy, and the well-known affection which
the brilliant young society dramatist felt for the actor, are
worth considering in any estimate that may be made of
Doggett's character.

One result of it may have been that the actor himself, as we
have seen, once tried his hand at authorship with very considerable
success. But it is the cause that will interest us most. We may
begin by taking a very considerable discount off the end of Tony
Aston's estimate of Doggett : "a lively, spract man, of very
good sense, *but illiterate*." This can scarcely be true of Congreve's
friend. There were few men then living but might have suffered
in the light of so brilliant a comparison ; yet we may at least

surmise that if there was one person the witty and eloquent writer would not have honoured with his friendship, it would have been an " illiterate " actor. However that may be, it is at least certain that as " Fondlewife," in *The Old Batchelor*, Doggett created a part that not only satisfied the writer of it, but retained the plaudits of the town for many years.

With the exception of *Love for Love* (in which Doggett had an equal success in another creation of his own, the part of " Ben ") it may perhaps be said that the comedies of Congreve are more suitable to the library than to the stage of the present generation, for as a painter of contemporary life and manners his supremacy is so astonishing that it obscures more lasting qualities. Yet there are particular scenes in *The Way of the World* which would no doubt contradict this generalization, could they be produced to-day with all the lightness of touch, in that exhilarating and witty atmosphere which seems inseparable from the radiant original.

The Old Bachelor was, by Dryden's confession, the finest " first play " he had ever seen. It may not indeed be so well done as other of Congreve's works, but it has no other equals in its own line ; and the art with which so much intoxicating dialogue was distributed among all that Drury Lane possessed of feminine charm and comic talent was only less than the genius of the play itself. Mrs. Bracegirdle spoke the prologue written by Captain Southerne, who had joined Dryden in making various technical suggestions for the stage production. When the same lovely actress appeared in the last act with Mrs. Barry (who spoke the daring epilogue), Mrs. Mountford and Mrs. Bowman, the audience were so struck with the sheer beauty of the group, that they burst into hearty and unpremeditated applause.

This Mrs. Barry was the daughter of a ruined Royalist who was first protected by Lady Davenant, and who owed her great theatrical popularity later on to the acquaintance and interest of Lord Rochester. Mrs. Mountford, a fair woman, " her face of a fine smooth oval," was a Miss Percival. Her first husband was killed by Lord Mohun for protecting Mrs. Bracegirdle, and

she then married Jack Verbrugen, who acted in several of Congreve's plays.

Mrs. Anne Bracegirdle, who is almost as well remembered as
Peg Woffington by the modern playgoer, was educated and cared
for like their own child by Betterton and his wife. She is
described by Colley Cibber as " the darling of the theatre ; for it
is no extravagant thing to say scarce an audience saw her that were
less than half of them her lovers." Two of her most popular
parts were " Statira " and " Millamant," and in Congreve she
seemed especially to find the parts that suited her, while the tale
may well be true that in the words he gave her stage-lovers Congreve expressed something of the admiration which he felt himself.

But I must not forget our hero, who managed to make his own
mark very clearly, even in the blaze of so much beauty. " Fondlewife," writes Steele, who saw the play on April 28, 1709, and
criticized it in the next *Tatler*, " is a lively image of the unreason-
able fondness of age and impotence." In the fourth act Doggett
made his appearance, as the foolish and uxorious old husband,
wrangling with his servant about the safety of his wife during his
short absence from home. The fun is broad enough, but when
" Cocky " comes out to see her " Nykin," and she stops his solemn
lecturing by sobs and kisses, the house must have been indeed
convulsed.

Need I say that he returns to find that the supposed Puritan,
Spintext, who had called upon Laetitia, was in reality the gallant
Bellamour, with " trusty Scarron's novels " for his prayer-book ?
The discovery, the confrontation, the utter turning of the tables
—these things should indeed be read (or seen) to be believed.
" Go to him, madam," cries Bellamour at last in a fine indignant
frenzy, " fling your snowy arms about his stubborn neck, bathe
his relentless face in your salt trickling tears." Of course " the
good man melts," and the spectacle of the befooled and bewildered
Doggett, with " kind nature working and boiling over in him,"
must have set the audience in a roar before the curtain fell.

Addison, in the *Spectator* for August 1, 1712, writing on the
subjects selected by playwriters of the time, has a remark about

Doggett which may well have been inspired by this celebrated part :

> If an Alderman appears upon the Stage, you may be sure it is in order to be Cuckolded. An Husband that is a little grave or elderly, generally meets with the same Fate. Knights and Baronets, Country Squires, and Justices of the Quorum, come up to Town for no other Purpose. I have seen poor *Dogget* Cuckolded in all these Capacities. In short, our English Writers are as frequently severe upon this innocent unhappy Creature, commonly known by the Name of a Cuckold, as the Ancient Comick Writers were upon an eating Parasite, or a vainglorious Soldier.

In July, 1710, Doggett chose the same part of " Fondlewife " for his benefit, for the comedy had evidently retained all the freshness of its deserved reputation, and he desired Steele's favour for that performance. " Doggett thanked me," records the *Tatler,* " for my visit to him in the winter, and after his comical manner, spoke his request with so arch a leer that I promised the droll I would speak to all my acquaintance to be at this Play." The incident is used by Steele to introduce the famous letter from Downes the prompter (supposed to be brought by Doggett on this occasion), in which Harley's newly formed Ministry was ridiculed. It was probably written by Anthony Henley and Temple Stanyan, while it is suggested that by Downes the prompter was meant Thomas Osborne, the first Duke of Leeds.

For publishing this letter, though he disavowed its authorship, Steele was deprived by Harley of his place as Gazetteer, which Swift (in his journal to Stella, October, 1710) says was worth a salary of three hundred pounds. The real John Downes was the author of *Roscius Anglicanus, or an Historical Review of the Stage,* which is still of value to all writers on the subject.

Congreve was fortunate enough to obtain a more immediate and substantial reward than any within the bestowal of Steele ; for directly *The Old Bachelor's* success was assured, Montagu gave him one Government position, and added the promise of another. The sparkling dialogue that won them both held the town too until 1789. A second play by the same dexterous hand, though deservedly not so popular, obtained the generous and magnificent tribute from Dryden which contained lines that Congreve never forgot. " Be kind," wrote the older poet to the coming star :—

CHELSEA CHURCH FROM BATTERSEA.

From an 18th Century print.

Be kind to my remains ; and, oh, defend
Against your judgment your departed friend.
Let not the insulting foe my fame pursue,
But guard those laurels which descend to you.

In 1695 appeared a play still better than either of its predecessors. To have reached, at twenty-five, the position which
Congreve had attained when *Love for Love* produced crowded
houses every night, is to have done more than most English writers
—even the greatest—had achieved at such an age in the opinion
of their own day. The success of the new play was so striking
that its happy and gifted author was commissioned to write a
fresh comedy every year (which he was far from doing) for the
new theatre which Betterton and other players from Drury Lane
had just opened on their own account in Portugal Row, Lincoln's
Inn Fields, in 1695. The epilogue reminds us that the actors
were giving their performance in what had been a tennis court :—

These walls but t'other day were filled with noise
Of roaring gamesters and your damn-me boys ;
Then bounding balls and rackets they encompass,
And now they're filled with jests, and flights, and bombast.

The lines were spoken by the fascinating Bracegirdle, who took
the part of " Angelica " when Steele reported the play for his
paper some fourteen years later. He describes the performance
on April 7, 1709, for the benefit of that " phoenix of the stage,"
Mr. Betterton, whom Pepys considered " the best actor in the
world."

" *Those excellent players,*" *says the first number of the* " *Tatler,*" " *Mrs. Barry,*
Mrs. Bracegirdle and Mr. Doggett, acted on that occasion. There has not been known
so great a concourse of persons of distinction as at that time ; the stage itself was covered
with gentlemen and ladies, and when the curtain was drawn it discovered even there a
very splendid audience. . . . All the parts were acted to perfection ; the actors were
careful of their carriage ; and no one was guilty of the affectation to insert witticisms
of his own, but due respect was had to the audience for encouraging this accomplished
player."

Doggett played the part of " Ben," and it is worth while to
contrast it more carefully with that of " Fondlewife " than I have
space to do here, in order to realize that an actor who could be a

great success in two such different characterizations, must have
been blessed with undeniable talent. For " Ben " is the very
antipodes of the maudlin old idiot in the older play, who is perhaps reflected in the doting and fatuous " Sir Sampson," a part
which Doggett might well have chosen had he not been equal to
creating a completely distinct personality. Ben rolls on to the
stage in the third act with a seaman's oath and more than a smack
of the sea in language and gesture. " I love to roam about from
port to port and from land to land," he tells Mrs. Frail ; " I
could never abide to be port-bound. Now a man that is married
has, as it were, d'ye see, his feet in the bilboes, and mayhap mayn't
get 'em out again when he would."

As might have been expected, he is not over-zealous when
confronted with the lady who is proposed as his partner for life
and proves as unwilling as her suitor. " Sea calf ! " he cries, " I
an't calf enough to lick your chalked face, you cheese-curd, you !
Marry thee ! 'oons, I'll marry a Lapland witch as soon, and live
upon selling contrary winds and wrecked vessels." His buoyant
and somewhat boisterous manners bring a refreshing whiff of
healthy brine into a company which stands in sore need of some
such ventilation. " Mayhap I have not so fair a face as a citizen
or a courtier ; but for all that I've as good blood in my veins, and
my heart as sound as a biscuit." You can almost hear the applause
as Doggett says the words across the footlights, with a smile at the
sympathetic pit. Ben has a song, too, of Buxom Joan, which
leads me to suspect our friend Thomas of a hitherto unnoticed
turn of voice[1]; and as the only sane man in a party who are either
" outright horn-mad," or feigning lunacy, he carries the sympathy
of audience and readers with him to the end.

In the 120th *Tatler* there is a letter from Mr. Thomas Doggett
announcing a performance of *Love for Love* for his own benefit,
and asking permission to publish on the bills that it was to be
given at the request of Isaac Bickerstaffe, Esq. He got a very

---

[1] In January, 1710, Doggett sang in one of the first Italian operas produced in
England, Buononcini's "Almanzos and Almahide, or the Conquest of Granada,"
the Second Part of which was written by Dryden.

courteous answer, in which that learned gentleman promised to
" come in between the first and the second act, and remain in the
right hand box over the Pit till the end of the fourth " ; and
Addison tells us later on that " a person dressed for Isaac Bickerstaffe did appear at the Playhouse on this occasion." Doggett
was no doubt helped by his lines, but he must have thoroughly
deserved an applause that lasted for so many years, until in 1717,
only four years before he died, he played the same part again
before his beloved Hanoverian, George I.

But Doggett's successes with Congreve were not, of course,
his only parts, though they are the only characters on which it is
here possible to enlarge at all. In 1696 he was " Young Hob "
in the only play he ever wrote, as I have mentioned before, *The
Country Wake.* That same year saw him as " Vaunter " in Lord
Lansdowne's *The Gallants,* and " Sapless " in Dilke's *Lover's Luck.*
Next season, " Mass Johnny " (a schoolboy) in Cibber's *Woman's
Wit* at Drury Lane, " Bull Senior " in *A Plot and No Plot,* and
" Learchus " in Vanbrugh's *Asop* were among the rôles in which
he was seen ; and about then he revisited Dublin for a short time,
and no doubt astonished Castle Street with the solid results of
his English reputation, soon after the Peace of Ryswick had given
European approval to the sovereignty of King William and the
succession of the Princess Anne. But it may be doubted whether
he left London during the period when the visit of Peter the
Great of Russia may well have caused a certain amount of fashionable visitation to the playhouses.

Another part we know he played was the comic " Shylock "
to Betterton's " Bassanio " in *The Jew of Venice,* Lord Lansdowne's
version of the *Merchant of Venice* which was performed in Lincoln's
Inn Fields. The part of " Moneytrap " in *The Confederacy,* a
comedy brought out by the Lincoln's Inn Company at Sir John
Vanbrugh's new theatre in the Haymarket, was one of his most
successful impersonations, and *Squire Trelooly,* the celebrated farce
in which Vanbrugh, Congreve and Walsh collaborated, largely
owed its success to Doggett's acting. While he was assisting
Cibber, Wilks and Swiney in the management of the Haymarket,

he played " Tom Thimble " in Buckingham's *Rehearsal,* a play
to be found in Arber's reprints, which anticipated the leading
motive of " The Critic " ; he was also to be seen as " Dapper "
in Ben Jonson's *Alchemist,* and as the " First Grave-digger " in
Hamlet. By 1713 he was managing Drury Lane with Collier and
Steele, and about that time he performed in Jonson's *Wife's Relief*
as " Sir Tresham Cash." The last part he created, on January
29 in that year, was " Major Cadwallader " in Charles Shadwell's
Humours of the Army. It is said that the last the public saw of
him was when he acted in *The Wanton Wife* for the benefit of
Mrs. Porter, but he does not seem to have appeared before an
audience after 1717, though he lived another four years, and his
three favourite parts, " Ben," " Fondlewife," and " Hob," were
often called for on various occasions during the twenty years of
his highest popularity.

Tributes to his talents and his native wit are numerous. " The
craft of an Usurer," writes Steele in the *Spectator,* " the Absurdity
of a rich Fool, the aukward Roughness of a Fellow of half-Courage,
the ungraceful Mirth of a Creature of half-Wit, might be for ever
put out of countenance by proper parts for Doggett." It will
be remembered, too, that when Addison is describing " The Trunk-
maker in the Upper Gallery," who always led the applause by
banging on the woodwork near him, he says that this energetic
lover of the playhouse had " broken half a dozen oaken Plants
upon Doggett." It is clear, in fact, that our friend " the famous
comedian " was of no slight account in the polite society of his
day as an actor of excellent parts and accomplished humour. By
more professional critics, and by his own colleagues, he was no less
appreciated. " Very aspectabund," writes Downes, " wearing a
farce on his face . . . the only comic original now extant." " The
most original of all his contemporaries," says Colley Cibber,
" his manner was his own . . . he could be extremely ridiculous
without stepping into the least impropriety . . . a prudent
honest man." " The most diligent, most laborious, most useful
actor seen upon the stage in a long course of years," asserted another who knew him well.

The net result is the picture of a clever actor, endowed by nature with a mirthful physiognomy; conscientious in using every extraneous aid to success, whether by careful dressing or by diligence in study; highly respectable, and a trifle opinionated, maintaining warmly, for instance, that comedy was superior to tragedy " because it was nearer to Nature " ; always keeping an eye upon the main chance, yet only obstinate when thwarted; but standing upon what he imagined to be his rights with absolute fearlessness ; a " theatrical patriot," in fact, as he has been rightly called, ever anxious to combat the least shadow of tyranny or unfairness ; a strong " politician " too, sometimes trailing a coat behind him, it may be suspected, for unwary managers to tread upon.

CHAPTER IV
Pugnacious Thomas

. . . Projicit ampullas et sesquipedalia verba . . .

THE most conspicuous example of this characteristic pug-
naciousness was found in the notorious dispute which
dissolved his long partnership with Wilks and Cibber. It has
been already noted that he was among those who protested
against their treatment by the managers of the Theatre Royal,
Drury Lane, and helped Betterton's new venture with
Congreve's plays in Lincoln's Inn Fields. But the breach
which was created by those successes of Booth to which I have
before referred was far more serious. In 1708 Swiny got
leave from the Lord Chamberlain to select by private treaty
certain actors from the Drury Lane Theatre to share with
him in the management of the Haymarket. Doggett was one
of them, and when Swiny retired he stayed on, successfully finding
the finances of the establishment with Wilks and Cibber. When
Booth's brilliant performance of " Cato " had won the favour
of the Tories and the promises of a Secretary of State, he was
admitted by Wilks and Cibber as another partner.

Doggett's objections may have been embittered by his furious
Whig proclivities, but in any case he risked the fact that their
licence was only held " during pleasure " and persisted in refusing
to countenance the new arrangement. He left the theatre,
and then demanded one-third of the profits as usual, although
Booth had by that time come in. He refused also either to set
a value on his own stock or to part with any of it, and the Vice-
Chamberlain appears to have supported him. Thereupon the
other partners were compelled to show fight. Doggett forth-

with filed a Bill in Chancery, and after two years of litigation was given fourteen days to decide what he would do. He stuck to his guns against his own interests, and on announcing his determination to quit the stage, he was decreed £600 for his share in the property, with fifteen per cent. interest since the date of Booth's admission, a very poor equivalent for the sum he might have made in the same time, had he agreed with his old friends and swallowed his political convictions.

I am tempted to quote here one of his letters to the Lord Chamberlain on April 17, 1714, as an example of his tenacity of purpose. It runs as follows, according to the original priced at £10 in a public auction only the other day :—

> I have obeyed all your commands, and from the assurance you was pleased to give me that I should have justice done me, I was persuaded to give you an account what money I had in my hands, and upon my doing so, I had your promise that the managers should be obliged in two days, that is to say on the Wednesday following, to bring in their account likewise and close with me, but I beg leave to remark to you, that it is now near six months since and I have not been able to obtain any account nor any manor of satisfaction, which I hope will excuse my taking such methods as shall be advised proper to come at my right. And as I have indeavour'd to show a just regard, Sir, to all your commands and omitted nothing that I thought was due from me to the office, I hope My Lord Chamberlain and Sir John Stanley will be satisfied that what I do is from necessity not choice.

By the kindness of Mr. A. M. Broadley, and of one of the Doggetts of Bristol, I am able to reproduce part of a letter written in January, 1714, on this same subject in Doggett's own handwriting, which shows (as does the signature to his will) that he spelt his name himself as I have printed it in these pages. Among Mr. Broadley's manuscripts there are also the original draft of a petition to the Lord Chamberlain, the Duke of Shrewsbury, in the matter of Rich and Drury Lane ; a memorandum in Doggett's own handwriting in which eleven very businesslike proposals as to the management of the theatre are submitted to the consideration of the Lord Chamberlain ; and a further memorandum concerning the dispute with Rich. But I have not thought it worth while to reproduce in full these evidences of bygone quarrels. The most amusing of them occurred in 1697, when

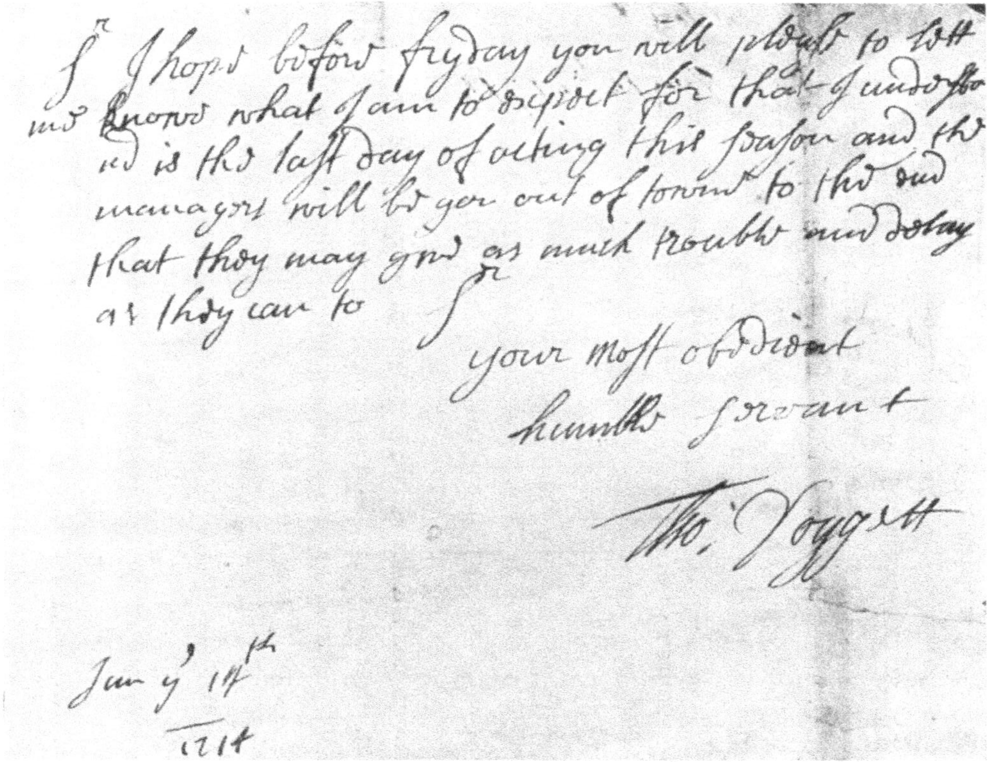

our pugnacious friend threw up his engagement in a rage and
went to Norfolk, whereon the patentee of the theatre in which
he had been acting under articles complained to the Lord Chamberlain, who sent a messenger down to bring back the actor.
Doggett's good humour on the drive to town, and the excellent
dinners he ordered all along the road at the expense of " the
Law," quite changed the opinions of the emissary as to the real
merits of the case ; and when sturdy Thomas reached London
he soon turned the laugh still more upon his own side, for he
appealed to Lord Chief Justice Holt for habeas corpus, and
fought the cause of the freedom of the stage with complete success.
Not only was he discharged, but the extravagance of the pro-
cess was severely censured. There had been nothing really
malicious in the sulks of Achilles in his tent at Norfolk. Doggett
may, in fact, be congratulated on the plucky stand he made against
the attempted encroachment of the authorities upon the rights
of actors.

But he certainly felt the quarrel created by the admission of
Booth to partnership, in his later years, far more deeply, and
his personal reconciliation with Cibber only took place after
" the principle of the thing " had been thoroughly vindicated.
For a long time visits to Button's coffee-house had been em-
barrassed by the indignant snorts and bellicose demeanour of the
wronged Irishman in presence of his oppressor. At last the
old dodge of a premature obituary notice was tried by a mutual
friend, and trusting Thomas fell into the snare like a child. He
came up to Button's and sat opposite Cibber, the writer. There
was a prolonged pause. At last Cibber tentatively offered a
pinch of snuff. " Humph," said the patriot cautiously, ". . . the
best—humph—I have tasted a great while." The ice thus diplo-
matically broken—(and where, it may be asked, is the diplomatic
snuff-box in these downright days ?)—Doggett proceeded to
explain that it was really Wilks who had been in fault. " I would
not be a Lord of the Treasury," he grumbled, " if such a temper
as Wilks's were to be at the head of it—a trifling wasp—a vain
shallow." No doubt he said much the same to Wilks of Cibber,

and at any rate his friends were loyal enough to his memory when the obituary notice was really needed.

Yet now that his plays have so long been over, and it is near two centuries since the last flicker of his oily footlights, by what is he remembered ?   By the skill with which he drew two opposite characters in Congreve's sparkling comedies ?   By the numberless parts he played with Betterton and Bracegirdle at Lincoln's Inn Fields, or the Haymarket, or Drury Lane ?   No.   But by a wager for Thames watermen in best and best boats upon the tideway.   Which of all our "famous comedians" of to-day are likely to leave a prize for sculling on the Thames ?   Not one, I fancy.   But then the Thames nowadays is not what it was to Mr. Thomas Doggett.

CHAPTER V

River Traffic and London Theatres

. . . Non aliter quam qui adverso vix flumine lembum
Remigiis subigit; si brachia forte remisit
Atque illum in praeceps prono rapit alveus amni." . . .

EVEN by Doggett's time Old London Bridge had been burned
down in the great fire. "Poor little Michell and our
Sarah" were on it, writes Pepys, who was wont sometimes to
take his morning draught, after the perils of getting through
the narrow piles, at that Old Swan Inn which perished in the
same great conflagration. But the "wine-shade" was probably
saved owing to its safer situation, for it is known to have been
let in 1697 for the convenience of citizens who "drank their
genuine old port and sherry, drawn from the casks, and viewed
the bridgeshooters and boatraces." It was most probably in
this genial company, as we shall see, that Doggett first made up
his mind to encourage boatracing by leaving a prize for young
watermen. The "shades" in which he sat were subsequently
removed to the house of Alderman Garratt, who, as Lord Mayor,
laid the first stone of the present London Bridge. The ancient
tavern above them has gone too. As long ago as 1323 it had
been left by one Rose Wrytell to trustees to maintain a priest
of the altar of St. Edmund, King and Martyr, and in the parish
book of St. Mary-at-Hill, under date 1499, the continuance of
her charity is proved. It was here that in 1440 Eleanor Cobham,
Duchess of Gloucester, landed, carrying a lighted taper, clad in
a white sheet and barefooted. The fifteenth century had seen
Henry V ride over the crowded arches of the old bridge, triumphing

after Agincourt. Beneath them he was borne on his bier to burial seven years later. So, in the next century, the body of the great Elizabeth was brought by water to Whitehall ; and so in the seventeenth, the twelve state barges of the City Companies escorted Charles II in state from Hampton Court.

The river in those days, and even long after Thomas Doggett's death, had a large share in the life of every Londoner. To remember it is to give some slight measure of our loss, in years when it seems likely to retire for ever beneath a tunnel of continuous bridges, in shame at having lost alike its usefulness for locomotion and its beauty for a pageantry of state.

The reason for Doggett's selection of his prize will become a little more intelligible after a closer consideration of the difference between his mode of life and ours ; and it may be remembered that if theatrical proprietors were interested, as we shall see, in the welfare of watermen, the watermen themselves were able to inspire Dibdin with a theme for his ballad-opera at the Haymarket, a work which, from the date mentioned in its title, may well have been suggested by one of the races for Doggett's Coat and Badge ; for it contains those celebrated ballads, originally sung by Tom Tug, which begin : " And did you never hear tell of a jolly young waterman " and " Farewell, my trim-built wherry." Verses that are not so well known, but that are just as certainly inspired (in the breast of some unknown poet of the Thames) by the same celebrated wager are :—

> Let your oars like lightning flog it,
> Up the Thames as swiftly jog it,
> An you'd win the Prize of Doggett
>   The glory of the River !
> Bending, bowing, straining, rowing,
> Perhaps the wind in fury blowing
> Or the Tide against you flowing
>   The Coat and Badge for ever !

But I am not sure that these lines were sung on the stage, and for the actual link between the theatre and the watermen I must at once go back to a still older actor whose career is in many ways a striking parallel to that of Thomas Doggett. For while there are many who are grateful for the foundation of Dulwich School, and while hundreds yearly know that Edward Alleyne founded it, there are not many who remember that Edward Alleyne, the friend of Ben Jonson, of Dekker, and of Heywood, "Proteus for shapes and Roscius for a tongue," was the builder of the Fortune Theatre, the popular actor of Marlowe's *Tamburlaine the Great*, the rival of Burbage (of the Globe), and the purchaser of Shakespeare's wardrobe and stock, for £596 6s. 8d., when the immortal writer left the Blackfriars Theatre and retired to Stratford-upon-Avon.

The connexion of the drama with watermen is for the first time really discoverable in an episode in Alleyne's life, in the year 1593, when the Plague had closed all the theatres, and even stopped, says Stowe, a few days of the merriment of St. Bartholomew's Fair. In that sad season, when the occupation of so many had been temporarily ruined, the Thames watermen sent a letter in the winter begging that the actors might be allowed to play once more. Their petition to "Lord Haywarde (i.e. Howard) Lord Highe Admirall of England" showed that Philip Henslowe (one of the groomes of Her Ma'ties chamber) had been restrained from playing, and that "we saide poore watermen have had much helpe and reliefe for us, oure poore wives and children, by means of the resort of suche people as come into the saide playhouse." This is signed by "Dowet, M^r of her M'ties barge," by two of Her Majesty's watermen, and by six other names ; and the playhouse referred to is the Rose, where Alleyne and Henslowe were joint actor-managers in the company known as "Lord Strange's Players."

Queen Elizabeth's patronage and encouragement of acting had made the dramatic profession much more serious and lucrative ; and it is evident that the existence of such theatres as the Blackfriars, Whitefriars, Hope, Rose, or Swan, had created a demand for traffic which the watermen supplied, and which the greatest architects were careful to consider, as when Sir Christopher Wren designed a "convenient landingstage" for the river frontage

A WATERMAN. EARLY 19TH CENTURY.
From the drawing by S. A. Atkinson.

of the Duke's Theatre in Dorset Gardens.[1] When the theatres were closed by royal edict, as sometimes happened from midsummer to Michaelmas, the watermen and actors suffered equally. At the present time the former are scarcely used by travellers

---

[1] In Randolph's *Muses' Looking-Glass* (1643) one of the characters utters a prayer—

> "That the *Globe*
> Wherein, quoth he, reigns a whole world of vice,
> Had been consumed, the *Phoenix* burnt to ashes,
> The *Fortune* whip't for a blind whore. *Black Fryers*
> He wonders how it 'scaped demolishing
> I' th' time of Reformation. Lastly he wished
> The *Bull* might cross the Thames to the *Bear Garden*
> And there be soundly baited."

Some of these old theatres have interesting histories. The one just mentioned in the text, as designed by Sir Christopher Wren, was built by Sir William Davenant in Salisbury Court, Fleet Street, and opened in 1671, with Betterton's Duke of York's Company. It was pulled down in 1709. The *Fortune* was built in 1599 by Alleyn and Henslowe and opened by the former with Lord Admiral Nottingham's servants, who had previously performed at the *Rose*, and who, in 1603, changed their patron for Henry Frederick, Prince of Wales. It was rebuilt, as Heywood describes it, in 1633, taken over by Dulwich College in 1649, and was still standing (though disused) in 1682.

Mr. Walter H. Godfrey has written a most interesting article on the original contract (1599–1600) for the building of the *Fortune* Theatre, which was brought to his notice by Mr. William Archer, and is preserved at Dulwich College. It was transcribed by J. O. Halliwell Phillipps in his *Outlines of the Life of Shakespeare*; but the chief value of Mr. Godfrey's essay is the light he throws, by the analysis of this document, upon that most controversial of all topics, the form of the Elizabethan stage. I must not stray so far from Doggett as to give Mr. Godfrey's results in these pages. My readers will find them in the *Architectural Review* for April, 1908. Visscher's drawing of London, in 1616, shows three buildings resembling amphitheatres, south of the Thames. These are the Elizabethan public theatres which were modelled on the old galleried inn yards, of which London itself had so many fine examples; and the *Fortune*, like them, was square, with three tiers of open galleries supported by posts. The audience all entered by one door leading into the open yard, and those who wished to go into the galleries had to pay a further sum for the privilege. There was a turret from which the trumpeter blew a signal to the people without that the play was about to commence.

The *Rose*, on Bank Side, Southwark, was built before 1590 and used by the companies of Lord Strange, the Earl of Sussex, and the Earl of Pembroke. It was forsaken by the actors in 1613, and we hear of prize-fights there (probably with the broadsword) in 1620. The *Hope* also stood on Bank Side in 1613, on the site of the old *Bear Garden*, pulled down earlier in the year, and there Ben Johnson's *Bartholomew Fair* was produced. Near the same spot were the *Swan*, which was closed in 1613, and used for prize-fighting in 1632, and the *Globe*. This latter was of wood with a roof of rushes, bearing on a turret a silken flag with the inscription " Totus mundus

at all, and the latter are consoled by playing to the provinces, a method of filling in the summer certainly known to Mrs. Siddons, but not to many of her predecessors. No such advice would now be given as was printed in *The Young Gallant's Academy* (1674–1696) to the following effect : " *Let us take a pair of oars for Dorset Stairs and so into the Theatre.*"

The number of watermen thrown out of employment in the old days when, for instance, the Thames was frozen over, may be judged from the calculation of Taylor, " the Water Poet," that no less than 40,000 plied for hire towards the close of the sixteenth century between Windsor and Gravesend. It is known from other sources that they could furnish 20,000 men for the fleet and had actually sent 8,000 on Her Majesty's ships. This means that, though their numbers gradually decreased, a far higher total than is often realized were affected by such social upheavals as civil war, hard frosts, or widespread visitations of disease.

Since its practical extinction in 1666, the Plague has become so shadowy a memory to Londoners, that we can scarcely conceive the dislocation of social life caused by such an outbreak as that which closed the theatres and lowered watermen's wages in 1593. As a matter of fact, it was never for long in abeyance in London for three centuries after the Black Death of 1348. It marred the coronation of James I by the deadly visitation of 1603. It wrecked the rejoicings at the accession of Charles I by the still more fatal epidemic of 1625. It only worked out the full venom of its hideous powers in the terrific outburst of 1665.

The pestilence of 1603 began in Stepney, which then extended

agit histrionem "—words which were afterwards used above the stage of Drury Lane. Shakespeare both wrote pieces for this theatre and played in them ; and on May 19, 1603, King James gave his royal licence to Lawrence Fletcher, William Shakespeare and others for plays " as well within theire usuall house, called the *Globe*, within our county of Surrey, as also within anie towne-halle. . . ." It was burnt down in 1613 owing to an accident after the discharge of cannon in Shakespeare's *Henry VIII*, and was rebuilt on larger lines next year on the north side of Maiden Lane.

from Shoreditch to Blackwall. The bustle and increase of business produced by the new reign gave it every chance of spreading. In June the Trinity law sessions were suspended. In July the nave of Old St. Paul's grew empty. The King's coronation procession extended only from the landing-stage at Westminster Bridge to the Abbey, for the deaths had risen to a thousand a week. The crowded and polluted alleys by the riverside were " vomiting their undigested dead." Most of the parish priests and nearly all the magistrates fled from the city. The places of reputable physicians were taken by a horde of ignorant and unscrupulous quacks. For a time all the wherries were hard at work transporting citizens into the country. But when the watermen returned to their usual stairs, it was to find one-sixth of the population buried, and all the theatres shut up.

In 1563, in 1577, as well as in 1593, the theatres had been closed. As though Providence were on the side of Shakespeare, his most active production of plays corresponded with a period of very remarkable abeyance of the Plague from 1594 to 1603, but for the following seven years the playhouse doors were far more often shut than open. Again there was a long period of freedom after 1610, only to be closed by the outbreak which heralded the accession of Charles I, fifteen years later. In 1648 Evelyn records that he " saw a Tragie-Comedy acted in the Cockpit, after there had been none of these diversions for many years during the warr." Here we find yet another reason for loss of traffic, apart from disease.

All these misfortunes in turn bore as heavily on the watermen as on " His Majesty's Poor Players " ; but when the theatre had widened its appeal far beyond court circles or the friends of the nobility ; when the appearance of actresses (whom Pepys saw for the first time in January, 1660) had provided a new and per-manent and regular feature ; when the stage, under Queen Anne, really began the popularity which has developed into modern dramatic attractions that are almost superfluously numerous ; then the watermen's wages rose from tens to hundreds, and we may imagine just such a connexion between them and the theatre

managers as exists between the modern cab rank and our later
dissipations. It must be remembered, too, that in 1710 the number
of licensed hackney-coaches was fixed at only 800, with fares at a
shilling for a mile and a half. There were, besides, only 200
licensed sedan-chairs at a shilling a mile ; and both these forms of
vehicle, usually without glass, had to bump over streets irregularly
paved with stone. On the river, though the boatmen were
sometimes rather rough, their craft were cushioned, and there
was shelter in the stern, so that the habit of " going by water,"
so common in the pages of *Pepys' Diary*, lasted for nearly a century
after his death, and was especially in favour for theatre parties.

In the *Spectator* for August 11, 1712, Steele gives a charming
description of the river life that has now so entirely vanished :—

When we first put off from Shore, we soon fell in with a Fleet of Gardeners
bound for the several Market-Ports of London ; and it was the liveliest Scene imaginable to see the Chearfulness with which these industrious People ply'd their way to
a certain Sale of their Goods. The Banks on each Side are as well peopled, and
beautified with as agreeable Plantations as any spot on the Earth ; but the Thames
it self, loaded with the Product of each Shore, added very much to the Landskip.
It was very easie to observe by their Sailing, and the Countenances of the ruddy Virgins
who were Supercargoes, the Parts of the Town to which they were bound. There
was an Air in the Purveyors for Covent Garden, who frequently converse with Morning Rakes, very unlike the seemly Sobriety of those bound for Stocks Market.

Nothing remarkable happened in our Voyage ; but I landed with Ten Sail
of Apricock Boats at Strand Bridge, after having put in at Nine Elms and taken in
Melons consigned by Mr Cuffe of that Place to Sarah Sewell and Company at their
Stall in Covent Garden.

Fifty years before, on his way by river from the Temple to
London Bridge, Pepys was told by White, his waterman, in February,
1660, that " the watermen had been lately abused by some that
had a desire to get in to be watermen to the State, and had lately
presented an address of nine or ten thousand hands to stand by
this Parliament, when it was only told them that it was a petition
against hackney-coaches. . . ." This shows that at any rate in the
middle of the seventeenth century the watermen had nothing
to fear, in point of numbers, from other forms of traffic ; and as a
matter of fact they drove a roaring trade, protected in many
different ways. Their fares had been regulated by Henry VIII ;

they were formed into a company by Philip and Mary in 1555 ; the Privy Council concerned itself with their pay ; the dimensions of their wherries, when " dangerously shallow and tickle " for passenger traffic, were regulated by a statute which clearly suggests to me the appearance of some young fellow with a light craft he fancied for a wager. How he would stare if he could see the winner's boat to-day !

Times have changed indeed ; and though Doggett's watermen can get faster from London Bridge to Chelsea than they ever did before, their trade in the passenger traffic has been ruined by the multiplication of bridges, and by all the new forms of locomotion which have been developing ever since the middle of the nineteenth century.

The Edward Alleyne, whose closed theatre caused the watermen so much distress, was leader of the Queen's Company of Players in 1583, and thus began a successful career which was not wholly taken up with things theatrical ; for in 1603 he and Henslowe were " Masters of the King's Games " and keepers of " the Mastiffes, Bandoggs," bears and other animals in what was then called Paris Garden, built on the present south approach of Blackfriars Bridge. Stowe's *Chronicle* gives a revolting description of " three of his fellest dogs " fighting a lion at the Tower, before James I, with his Queen and the Prince. The post brought them in £500 a year ; but Alleyne must have made much more by his theatres ; for in 1596 he is recorded to have sold a single estate in Essex for £3,000, a large sum in those days ; and it is perhaps significant of his personal inclinations that in 1614, though still " Master of the Games," he was using the Paris Garden for producing plays. It may well be to some such " theatre " as this that Shakespeare refers in the well-known lines,

> Can this cockpit hold
> The vasty fields of France ? Or may we cram
> Within this wooden O the very casques
> That did affright the air at Agincourt ?

By the time he had reached the age of forty-seven, Alleyne realized that he had large estates and no family to whom to leave

THE RACE FOR DOGGETT'S COAT AND BADGE. NEAR THE MIDDLE OF THE COURSE.

From the original by Rowlandson in the possession of Mr T. A. Cook.

them. So he determined to found God's Gift College at Dulwich, and began it, as some say, under the direction of Inigo Jones, in 1613. Francis Bacon, who opposed Sutton's efforts to found the Charterhouse, was equally unsympathetic, and fortunately equally unsuccessful, when Alleyne applied for a Charter for his scholastic foundation; and Dulwich College exists to-day as one of the best memorials an actor ever left. It benefited, curiously enough, from the legacy of another actor in the seventeenth century, William Cartwright, one of Killigrew's Company after the Restoration, who left the College his books, his furniture, and pictures, among which is his portrait.

Thus comes it, then, that the memory of Edward Alleyne is enshrined with his bones at Dulwich. It is indeed a splendid monument, and more desirable, to my mind, than many a sculptured platitude within the Abbey walls; but I doubt whether it will cope with Doggett's. Both have vanquished the oblivion inherent in their art by connecting their names with institutions that endure. Why Doggett, the actor, chose a waterman's wager to perpetuate his memory has become clearer, I think, from the revelation now established of the kindly feeling on both sides. His gift was very natural; and in the later eighteenth century the following notice issued by the proprietors of the Royal Coburg Theatre shows that other lovers of the stage besides Doggett saw the propriety of taking a similar course, but wisely did so before they had passed beyond the possibility of benefiting by their shrewdness :—

To the Watermen of Blackfriars and Waterloo Bridges, the Proprietors have great pleasure in announcing that as a reward for their past as well as future attention to the Public, Sir Thomas Wilson Bart. early in the ensuing October will give A PRIZE WHERRY. The particulars of the arrangement will be duly announced. The winner to receive the boat on the stage of the Royal Coburg Theatre.

Neither this instance nor the munificence of Thomas Doggett was the only one of the kind recorded. The proprietor of Cupar's Gardens gave a prize-wherry every year. So did Philip Astley and Edmund Kean. In 1730 a sporting lady living in Battersea, who may be strongly suspected of the footlights, gave a scarlet coat to be rowed for by six apprentices of five years' standing. The connexion between the river and the stage lasted, in fact, until the era of multiplied bridges and the Metropolitan Railway. But no other kindly evidence of that connexion, except Doggett's wager, has ever stood the test of time. His race has survived because he took care that the last lines of the famous placard of 1716 should be no empty boast. " They are to row," we read, " from London Bridge to Chelsea. It will be continued annually on the same day *for ever*." With just the same phrase Baddeley bequeathed his Twelfth Night cake and wine for " the ladies and gentlemen of Drury Lane." Yet there are not many of us who read of that annual hospitality, not many even among those partaking of it, who remember that Robert Baddeley, the last actor who showed his pride in being a " King's servant " by wearing the royal uniform of gold and scarlet, created the part of " Moses " in " The School for Scandal." He knew we should not think of that. He determined that his Cake, at any rate, should last " for ever," a pathetic recognition, as it seems to me, of the truth that we should only recall the forgotten actor in thinking of his generous bequest.

But Doggett was of an earlier age ; and I fancy I can recognize a quiet confidence about the words " for ever " that is characteristic of the man. The curious thing is that they hold true to-day, nearly two hundred years later. It is time to look more closely, if we can, at the personality of so accurate a prophet.

CHAPTER VI

Off the Stage

Erat Homo ingeniosus, acutus, acer, et qui plurimum et salis haberet et fellis, nec candoris minus.

AS far as I can discover, no biography of Thomas Doggett has ever been separately published. Though it is comparatively easy to unearth the official traces of a successful dramatic career from contemporary records of the Stage, the business becomes much more complicated when details in the private life of a man who died childless in 1721 have to be discovered for the first time " for print." Only one relative (an Irish niece) is mentioned in his will ; and the only gentleman I know out of the many who bear his name to-day possesses no proof of direct descent from the same family.

This gentleman, Mr. John Thomas Doggett, of London, is of the family of Thomas Doggett, of Upwell in Cambridgeshire, whose arms are gules, two greyhounds, salient, combatant, collared sable. By his kind offices a book was lent to me, for the purpose of these researches, entitled *A History of the Doggett-Daggett Family,* by Samuel Bradlee Doggett, a member of the New England Historical and Genealogical Society, who has very kindly written to me from the United States conveying a very courteous expression of his interest in these pages. His book, which is a bulky compilation, was published (in 300 copies) at the press of Rockwell & Churchill in Boston, U.S.A., and the majority of its many entries are concerned with the various American branches of the family. There are four branches traceable in Ireland, two of them in Dublin. Other branches are traced in London, Yorkshire, Norfolk, Suffolk (Boxford and Groton), Bedfordshire,

Surrey, Somerset, Middlesex (Stoke), Hertfordshire, and Manchester.

The name Doggett, with its variants, Duckett and Daggett, is evidently very old. The suggestion that it is derived from "Dowgate" I cannot accept; but from the occurrence of greyhounds in the arms it seems likely that there was originally some connexion with "dog." Professor John Marshall Doggett, of Richmond, Virginia, does not, however, admit that in this case the word "dog" refers to the animal. He derives the name from the Aryan root dok or dog, which is discoverable in such words as dogma, doge, Doug-las, docket, dogger.

One of the earliest forms of the name is Duchet, anglicized into Ducket. It was spelt Doget in Lincolnshire and Norfolk, but occurs as Doggett in Elizabethan records; and since it is this latter form which Thomas Doggett, our "famous Comedian," uses for signing his letters and his will, I have printed his name as "Doggett" in these pages.

The name occurs in the early records of the City; for John Doget, born in London in 1240, is mentioned in 1277 as a "taverner" in the reign of Edward I, and in 1456 a vintner named John Doggett was buried in St. Leonard's, Eastcheap. But the family can soon boast of more distinguished sons; for in 1481 John Doggett was elected from Eton to King's College, Cambridge; he became Provost of King's in 1499; and was buried in Salisbury Cathedral. In 1509 a John Doget was Sheriff and Alderman of London. Another interesting fact is that Shakespeare, who died in 1616 at Stratford-on-Avon, had lived there in a house built by Sir Hugh Clopton, whose family monuments are at Melford, Suffolk; and it was a Margaret Clopton (who also died in 1616) who had married Thomas Doggett at Groton in Suffolk.

The Doggetts are certainly an old family in Ireland, and may have had an even more respectable origin than that of Dennis O'Kelly, the capable adventurer who came to England just as penniless as our hero, made an even bigger fortune, and is equally certain of immortality in sporting circles, owing to his ownership of the famous horse Eclipse whose son won the second Derby,

and transmitted his extraordinary excellence to the greater pro-
portion of all the thoroughbreds who have won the Derby ever
since.

The founder of the Watermen's Derby—for " Doggett's
Coat and Badge " deserved no lesser appellation—was probably
a descendant of the " Dogoit " or " Doget " quoted in Gilbert's
History of Dublin from Anglo-Irish annals of the thirteenth century,
and a certain " Gilbertus Doget " is mentioned in connexion
with Dublin in an unpublished Pipe Roll of that time. But
our hero was only the son of a small tradesman, and even the date
of his birth in Castle Street, Dublin, is not accurately discoverable.
Some authorities give it as 1670, but I am inclined to place it
earlier, for he is known to have died in 1721, and there are indica-
tions that he was older than fifty at his death. It is also known
that he married Mary Owen ; and if the manuscript in the British
Museum (Add. MSS. 27–466–203–613) called " Mary Doggett
Her Book of Receits 1682 " is correctly dated, and refers to his
wife, he must have been more than twelve years old when he
married her. Whether his first appearance in this country was
made at Bartholomew Fair or not, he was certainly acting at
Drury Lane in 1691, a fact which does not look very much like
the youth and inexperience of barely twenty-one. It may further
be suggested that as he is known to have acted before he left
Ireland, he would only have come to England to get better pay
if he had realized that his talents were insufficiently recognized
in his own country, and this realization in itself would imply a
certain experience of the stage and a certain mental balance,
which takes time to acquire.

On the whole, my conclusion, based on the various hypotheses
which are all we have to guide us, would be that our Thomas
Doggett was born nearer 1650 than 1670 ; that he married Mary
Owen at Eltham, in Kent, when he was about thirty and had made
up his mind that he could win an honest livelihood in England ;
and that his appearance at Drury Lane in 1691 was the result
not merely of a couple of years or so trial performances at Bartholomew's Fair, but of some ten years' experience in travelling

companies in various parts of England. This would not be at
variance with the supposition (mentioned in my second chapter)
that it was in 1689 or 1690 he came to the definite conclusion not
to act again, in permanent engagements, in Dublin ; for he is
known to have revisited Ireland occasionally, and it may well
have been the troubles with Tyrconnel that finally decided him
to make his home in England where he had already chosen his
wife. It would also make him about seventy when he died.

Evidently a contemporary observer is correct in the supposition
that the youthful Thomas had " to fight a passage through the
rough shambles of life as best he could." Luckily he was quite
equal to the fray, but the marks of the struggle are traceable
in certain characteristic idiosyncrasies already noted in his subse-
quent career.

I have mentioned various descriptions, most of them highly
creditable to our hero, which have been left of him by contemporary writers of repute. A more intimate portrait is given by
one of his companions, Anthony Ashton, the " Tony Aston "
of my previous pages. In this he is described as :—

*in person a lively little man ; in behaviour modest cheerful and complaisant. He
sang in company very agreeably and in public very comically. He danced the Cheshire
Round full well as Captain George. I travelled with him in his strolling company and
found him a man of very good sense . . . he dressed neat and something fine, in plain
cloth coat and a brocaded waistcoat, while I travelled with him each sharer kept his horse,
and was everywhere respected as a gentleman.*

In the records of Watermen's Hall there are a few more details
which may help us to imagine him:—

He wore an enormous wig with long lappets of hair hanging over his shoulders
which enveloped his head, and on the top of it was stuck a small cocked hat which
it would have been a great effort of balancing to retain in its place without the aid
of pins. His coat, very broad on the tails, reaches below his knees, his waistcoat,
with flap pockets of large size, extends half way down his thighs. His small-clothes
are light and buckled at the knees, where they are met by coloured stockings which
rise out of square-toed, red-heeled, silver-buckled shoes. Under his left arm he
carries a clouded or amber-coloured cane, while his right hand is continually titillating
his olfactory nerve with snuff from out of a box set with precious stones, and the
indispensable rapier hangs at his side.

After comparing this with Tony Aston's phrases, I confess
that the vast wig, the tiny hat, the constant snuff-box suggest

a character on the stage rather than the living portrait of the man whose career has been described in previous pages. I am inclined, in fact, to apply to the writer that quotation from Cicero which Steele sets at the head of one of his *Spectator* papers in a year when Doggett was at the zenith of his fame : " Voluisti enim in suo genere unumquemque nostrum quasi quendam esse Roscium . . ." Doggett was not always an actor, and indeed from certain events with which he is connected I suspect him to have shrewdly taken to heart the lines of Horace which appear above another essay in the *Spectator*, published only six weeks after the House of Hanover had succeeded to the throne of England :—

> . . . solutos
> Qui captat risus hominum, famamque dicacis,
> Fingere qui non visa potest, commissa tacere
> Qui nequit, hic niger est, hunc tu, Romane, caveto.

Doggett would never have been so much a favourite with the Romans of his day had he not been able at will to exchange the drolleries and deceptions of the footlights for the sound common sense, the sturdy, independent, honourable rectitude which marked his private life. I wish I knew more of it. Here and there, in the writings of the period, you find a more personal note, like that of Tony Aston's. There is Dibdin's opinion, for instance :—

> The Acting of Doggett was so chaste and his manners in private life so well bred that *he never chose to be the actor anywhere but on the stage*, yet his company was warmly sought after by persons of rank and taste.

This seems to me much more the real man, and I quote it from the Catalogue Raisonnée of Mr. Matthews' Gallery of Theatrical Portraits from 1659 onwards, which were first exhibited in 1833 at the Queen's Bazaar in Oxford Street. This catalogue is preserved by the Garrick Club ; and from it, number 55, described as " Thomas Doggett, Actor, Dramatist, and Patentee," is the picture that now hangs on the club walls. Unfortunately there is no real proof that it represents Doggett ; and it is as different as possible from the description in the records of Waterman's Hall. In the Garrick Club picture, excellently painted, you see a fat, strong, good-humoured face ; a large nose, somewhat

tip-tilted ; a clean-shaved, mobile lip above a well-formed chin
that threatens soon to become double. He is draped in a dark-
coloured cloak of fine material, with lace ruffles at his neck and
at the wrist of a particularly well-formed, capable, and expressive
hand. The wig has nothing of the enormous ; no " long lappets
of hair " hang over his shoulders. No " small cocked hat " is
stuck ridiculously on its summit. The man looks a respectable,
middle-aged gentleman with a witty countenance, and a fit com-
panion for any gentleman of his day and generation ; certainly
not a personage who imagined that the motto " Totus Mundus
Agit Histrionem " should be carried from its proper place, across
the top of Drury Lane stage, into social or domestic circles.

The only portrait with any pretensions to authenticity which
I have been able to discover is the one I have reproduced from
Daniel's *Merrie England* an engraving after a painting formerly
preserved at Lynne Regis in Norfolk, which represents Doggett
dancing the " Cheshire Round," one of the most popular of his
accomplishments. Though the Garrick Club picture would
be more useful for my argument, I see nothing in the less skilful
engraving which would lead me to consider it impossible as a
portrait of the man whom Dibdin praised so sympathetically.
If Doggett knew when to be an actor, he also knew how to play
the man. He never mixed the parts.

Among the few things about Doggett which have yet come
to light is the fact that when he left the stage, some time about
1714, he retired to Eltham, where he had some sort of home and
family before. It might be thought that Pepys' delightful pages
would have contained some personal reference to him among
the many notes on theatres. But though the busy Secretary of
the Admiralty lived till 1703, the last entry in the famous *Diary*
was written long before Doggett ever acted at Drury Lane ; and
Evelyn, though his entries are scrupulously kept up till within
three weeks of his death in 1706, has no mention of the actor.
It is different with Addison (Addison of Charterhouse and Queen's),
who died in 1719, the year when Booth married Hester Santlow.
But both this essayist and Steele were concerned with Doggett

rather as material for dramatic criticism than as a personality. So I am reduced to the Parish Registers of Eltham.

From these, and from the researches of local historians, it appears that Doggett married Mary, the granddaughter of Dr. Richard Owen, a divine somewhat celebrated in his day, who was ejected, owing to his Royalist proclivities, from the living of Eltham in 1643, given the living of North Cray in 1657, and created Doctor of Divinity and Prebend of St. Paul's in 1660. No inconsiderable man, in fact. He died at Eltham and was buried there on January 27, 1682, and his wife Amy was laid beside him twelve years afterwards, leaving her " granddaughter, Mary Doggett, all my plate and jewels." A little calculation will show that this granddaughter, if she were the " Mary Doggett " of the British Museum manuscript, might have easily been twenty-five or more if she was the wife of Thomas Doggett in 1682, the date of her " Book of Receits," and if so, she did not survive her husband, for there is no mention of her (or any other wife) in his will.

Taking these dates into consideration, we may also deduce the fact that Doggett was not married at Eltham, but that he dwelt there afterwards because his wife's family had had so long a connexion with the place. It is sad to think that his wife lived only a very short time after his retirement, and was buried near her father's grave. He was himself interred in the vault of the Parish Church on September 27, 1721, and the entry of his burial still exists in the Parish Registers. I have no proof that he married again, or that he had any children, and it is therefore natural that he should have applied a small part of his comfortable fortune to the foundation of his famous wager.

The origin of this race is, fortunately, more the business of my experienced collaborator than my own. But I must suggest one instance of the dangers and another of the amusements connected with watermen just before Doggett's time. The first occurs in the decorous memoirs of John Evelyn.

" I returned home," he writes, " on the 19th of January, 1649, passing an extraordinary danger of being drowned by our wherries falling foule in the night on another

DOGGETT DANCING THE CHESHIRE ROUND.

vessell then at anker, shooting the bridge at 3 quarters ebb, for which His mercy
God Almighty be praised."

Three days after the river was frozen over, so an upset would
have been undoubtedly unpleasant. The difficulty of passing
London Bridge is again emphasized by a sentence or two in *Pepys'*
Diary for May 18, 1661, and I cannot but think that here we
have something like a *locus classicus* for such a race as Doggett's ;
at all events we may with certainty consider that the diarist
refers to one of the many haphazard contests which Doggett
crystallized into a single substantial and permanent wager. The
passage runs as follows :—

> *Was fain to stand upon one of the piers about the bridge, before the men could drag
> their boat through the lock . . . being through bridge I found the Thames full of boats
> and galleys and upon inquiry found there was a wager to be run this morning. So spying
> of Payne in a gally, I went in to him, and there staied, thinking to have* GONE TO CHELSY
> *with them. But upon the start the wager boats fell foul of one another, till at last one of
> them gives over, pretending foul play, and so the other row away alone and all our sport
> lost.*

Whereupon I have no doubt the excellent Secretary went to
the "Old Swan," and, as he had done the year before, consoled
himself with " two or three quarts of wine, very good, and 200
walnuts." But this disappointment of his clearly refers to a wager
to be rowed in wherries by watermen from London Bridge to
Chelsea against the tide ; and these are almost precisely the original
conditions of Thomas Doggett's race.

I can find myself no records of this race before the notice
already quoted for the wager of 1716. But the records of Watermen's Hall seem to imply that there was a race in 1715, for they
relate that in this year :—

> *On the first of August, Thomas Dogget, comedian, a great Whig in Politics, lately
> joint manager of Drury Lane Theatre with Wilks and Cibber, gave a coat and badge
> to be rowed for by six watermen in the first year of their freedom.* IT WAS ROWED FOR
> ON THIS DAY, BEING THE FIRST ANNIVERSARY OF THE ACCESSION OF KING GEORGE I.

There are certain inaccuracies in the first line of this paragraph
which lead me to suspect the date given in the last. Though
Doggett was managing Drury Lane in 1713, he was not there in
1714, and had probably retired by then. For he had become
a partner of Cibber, Wilks and Swiny at the Haymarket (not

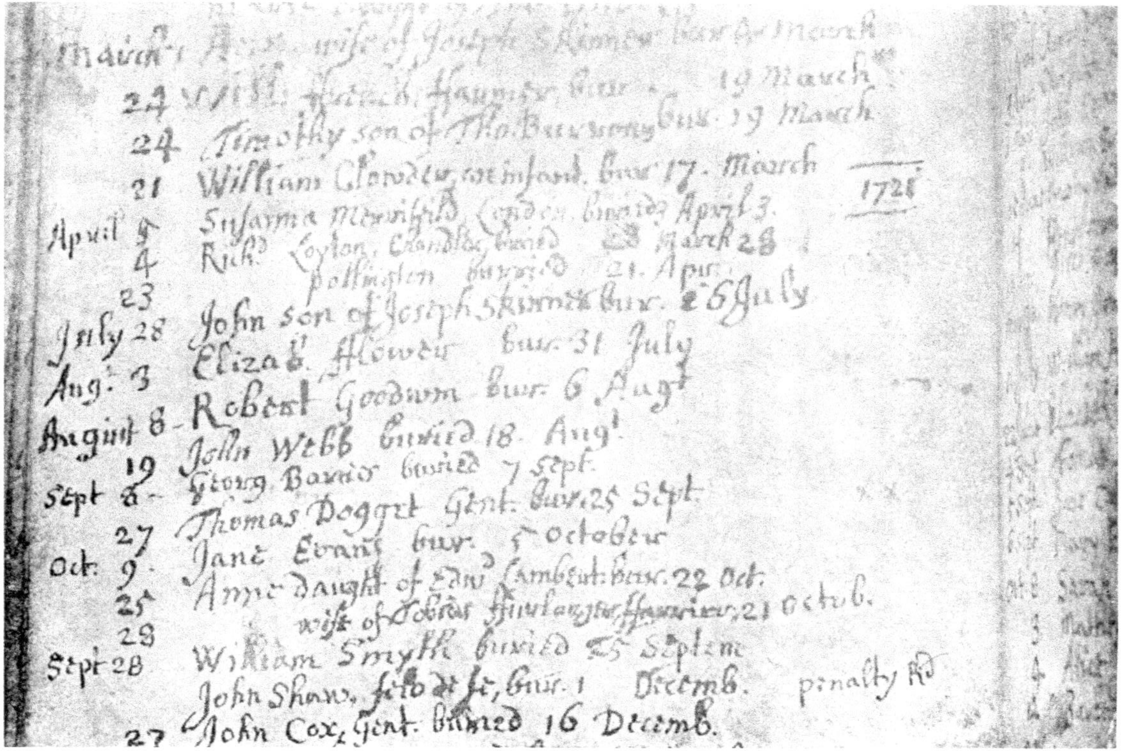
March 1 [illegible] wife of Joseph Skinner bur. [illegible] March
24 [illegible] Haynes bur. 19 March
24 Timothy son of Tho. [illegible] bur. 19 March
21 William [illegible] bur. 17. March
April 5 Susanna [illegible] buried April 3. 1728
4 Rich.d [illegible] Chandler buried March 28
[illegible] buried 21. Apr.
23
July 28 John son of Joseph Skinner bur. 26 July
Aug. 3 Eliza.th Flower bur. 31 July
August 8 Robert Goodwin bur. 6 Aug.t
19 John Webb buried 18 Aug.t
Sept 8 Georg. Barnes buried 7 Sept.
27 Thomas Dogget Gent. bur. 25 Sept.
Oct. 9 Jane Evans bur. 5 October
25 Anne daught. of Edw.d Lambert bur. 22 Oct.
28 [illegible] wife of [illegible] 21 Octob.
Sept 28 William Smyth buried 25 Septem.
John Shaw, felo de se, bur. 1 Decemb. penalty [illegible]
27 John Cox, Gent. buried 16 Decemb.

Register of Burials at Eltham Church.

Drury Lane) by 1708, and only left them when they took in Booth as a partner after the success of Addison's *Cato*, the first night of which was April 14, 1713, at Drury Lane; and the *Spectator* for the following year has several references to its more celebrated passages. I therefore incline to think that, unless an indisputable winner for 1715 can be found—and it is improbable that the first winner should be almost the only one unknown—the race was regularly instituted only in 1716, the year before Doggett's last appearance in public at a benefit performance.[1] The record in Watermen's Hall, which shows other signs of having been "written up" some time after the events mentioned, goes on as follows :—

The match seems to have been continued annually during his life. He died on September 22, 1721, endeared to Whigs and watermen, and was buried in the churchyard of St. John the Evangelist, Eltham, Kent, having by his will dated September 10, 1721, hereinafter referred to, provided for the perpetual continuance of the match.

The Will, proved on October 2, 1721, runs as follows :—

This is the last Will and Testament of me Thomas Doggett of the Parish of St. Paul's Covent Garden in the County of Middlesex, Gentleman, made this Tenth day of September Anno Domini One Thousand seven Hundred Twenty and one.

Imprimis. I give and bequeath the Sum of One Thousand pounds unto Twenty poor men (to be chosen by my Executors herein after named) who are ffreemen of and are or have been Shop keepers in the City of London and who were never respectively worth ffifty pounds in the Stock of their severall Trades that is to say to each one of the said twenty poor Men ffifty pounds.

Item. I give unto my Kinsman Captain Jacob Hallister of Bristol the Sume of Two Hundred pounds and my Gold Watch.

Item. I give unto Mrs Mary Peck of Eltham in Kent Widow the Sume of One Hundred pounds.

Item. In case my Niece Mary Young continues alive and in Ireland at my Death Then I give to her the Sume of Two Hundred Pounds.

Item. I give to my Servant Ann Gibbons the Sume of Thirty Pounds per annum during her natural Life to be paid Quarterly at the four usual Quarter days in the year the ffirst payment to be made on such of the said Quarter days as shall happen next after my decease; I further give unto the said Ann Gibbons the Sume of Twenty Pounds for Mourning and all my Cloathes and wearing Apparel, Linnen and Wollen and my Household ffurniture.

Item. I give unto Catherine Gibbons Sister of the said Anne the sume of Ten pounds.

---

[1] The only evidence in favour of 1715 has been brought to my knowledge by Mr. John T. Doggett. The *Weekly Journal* for Saturday, August 15, 1715, prints the following : "Monday last six Watermen who were scullers, rowed from London Bridge to Chelsea. . . ." When asked his opinion as to this reference, the Editor of *Notes and Queries* (April 16, 1864) replies that it was the race for Doggett's Coat and Badge; but gives no reason for this assertion.

Item. I give unto Mrs Mary Reynolds, wife of Thomas Reynolds Esqr one of my Executors herein after appointed my best Diamond Ring.

Item. It is my Will and I do hereby direct that my Executors shall forthwith by and out of my personal Estate purchase ffreehold Lands of inheritance to the value of Ten pounds per Annum and to cause such Lands when purchased to be conveyed unto Edward Burt of the Admiralty office, Esqr his Heirs and assignes subject to and charged and for ever Chargeable with the laying out ffurnishing and procuring yearly on the ffirst day of August for ever the following particulars that is to say, ffive pounds for a Badge of Silver weighing about twelve ounces and representing Liberty to be given to be rowed for by Six young Watermen according to my Custom, Eighteen Shillings for Cloath for a Livery whereon the said Badge is to be put, one pound one shilling for making up the said Livery and Buttons and Appurtenances to it and Thirty shillings to the Clerk of Watermens Hall All which I would have to be continued for ever yearly in Comemoration of his Majesty King George's happy Accession to the Brittish Throne.   The Remainder of the Rents and profitts of the said Lands when purchased I give and bequeath unto the said Edward Burt his Heirs and Assignes for ever.

And in the meantime until such purchase I direct my Executors to ffurnish the said Badge Livery and other things in manner aforesaid upon every ffirst day of August that shall happen.

I desire that my Body may be decently buried in like manner as my late Wife was, both as to privacy and Expence.

Item. I give devise and bequeath unto my very good ffriends Sir George Markham of the Temple Baronett and Thomas Reynolds of South Minns in the County of Middlesex, Esqr. All my South Sea Stock, Subscripcons and Bonds All my Cash, Jewells, plate, Goods and Effects whatsoever not hereinbefore disposed of.   And all the rest and residue of all my Estate reall and personal of what nature or kind so ever and wheresoever to the proper use and benefit of them the said Sir George Markham and Thomas Reynolds Executors of this my Will [1] And I hereby revoke and declare void all former and other Wills or Testaments by me at any time heretofore made And do declare this present Writing to be my last Will and Testament.

IN WITNESS WHEREOF I have hereunto Sett my hand and Seal the **Tenth** day of September Anno Domini One Thousand Seven hundred Twenty and one above menconed.   THO: DOGGETT.

Signed sealed published and declared by the before named Thomas Doggett for and as his last Will and Testament in the presence of us who have hereunto Subscribed our names as Witnesses in his presence.

JOHN BILTON, fferdn JOHN PARIS.

Proved 2 October, 1721. (Somerset House, " Buckingham," 177.)

From the minute provisions made in this document, it will be fully realized how careful was friend Doggett himself that his wager should be " continued annually on the same day for ever." His executors, as we shall see, were equally conscientious.

---

[1] In the margin opposite to this part the following words are written : " the said Sr George Markham and Thomas Reynolds their Heirs Executors Administrators and assigns for ever, their first paying all my Debts Legacys and ffuneral Expences, I do hereby constitute and appoint."

CHAPTER VII

Doggett's Bequest

Divisum sic breve fiet opus.

FURTHER details of Doggett's gift to the watermen are to be found in a place which at first sight does not seem to have much connexion with either party; for it is in Fishmongers Hall that is preserved the Agreement in their Will Book by which that Ancient and Honourable Company now carry out the intention of Doggett's bequest.[1]

This Tripartite Indenture (witnessed by John Linton, James Porter and Matthew Tanner) is dated November 29, 1721, in the eighth year of George I, and is made between Edward Burt of the Admiralty Office of the first part, and the Warden and Commonalty of the Mistery of Fishmongers of the second part, and Sir George Markham of the Temple, Baronet, and Thomas Reynolds of South Minns in the County of Middlesex, Esquire, executors of the will of Thomas Doggett, late of St. Paul's, Covent Garden in the County of Middlesex, Gentleman, of the third part. WHEREAS by Thomas Doggett's will dated 10 September 1720 certain freehold lands were to be purchased to be conveyed to Edward Burt of the Admiralty Office his heirs and assigns to the value of £10 per annum for ever chargeable with furnishing yearly £5 for the Badge of silver of twelve ounces representing Liberty to be rowed for by six young watermen according to the said Thomas Doggett's custom, with eighteen shillings for cloth for a livery (orange-coloured, of course, at first, though changed afterwards) whereon the badge is to be put, twenty-one shillings for making up the livery, its buttons and appurtenances, and thirty shillings

---

[1] Neither Doggett nor his executors were Freemen of the Company. Mr. Burt was not a Freeman.

to the Clerk of Watermen's Hall; it seems to the executors that the best way of performing Thomas Doggett's intention will be to repose the trust of performing the same in the Mistery of Fishmongers.

The result of this preamble, shorn of legal superfluities, is that in consideration of the sum of £350 the aforesaid Fishmongers' Company promised to pay 30s. to the Clerk of the Watermen's Company for registering, nominating and certifying six watermen, free of the said Company and duly qualified as Thomas Doggett settled; and to provide a silver badge " with the impress of a Wild Horse (of Hanover) as Thomas Doggett used in his life," with inscription round it, to be rowed for, with a coat, every year by six duly certified young men free of the said Company of Watermen on the first August (if a Sunday, then on the Monday following) for ever, the Warden and Commonalty of Fishmongers acting as judges and directors of the race, and appointing both start and finish. These are the Old Swan wharf at London Bridge, and the site where the Swan at Chelsea formerly stood, and the limits are probably much the same as they have always been, though the conditions under which we see the contest are different indeed. But it remains the best test on the river of skill in rough water and good steering. In the British Army the motto that appertains to the badge of " The White Horse of Hanover " is always " Nec aspera terrent." The words have a singularly apt application to the winners of that badge in Doggett's race.

On that August afternoon, in 1722, when Doggett's immortality really took its rise, the sturdy old actor had been buried at Eltham for almost twelve months. Addison was dead, but Pope, Defoe and Steele were still ministering to the entertainment or instruction of their countrymen, and Swift was not yet silent. Men had not quite forgotten the great crash which followed the bursting of the South Sea Bubble. Craig, the Secretary of State, had died of terror at the investigations. Amid the general wreck of all his rivals Walpole had risen again to power, and in 1721 had been again made First Lord of the Treasury, with Townshend as Secretary of State. Men were as used to news of fighting in the field as we are. The Turks were harassing Venice. The war of the Spanish Succession was in full blast. In our American Colonies Carolina's Governor had just been struggling for life with " the merciless Indian savage," and the buccaneers of the West Indies had received a sharp lesson from New Providence. Politicians at home were all discussing the prospects of the second Parliament of George I, which would meet in two months' time. I am not sure that we think much more of that excellent monarch to-day than we do of Mr. Thomas Doggett, but the race one started in honour of the other still goes on " in commemoration of the happy accession of the family of His Present Majesty to the Throne of Great Britain," as the loyal Fishmongers of to-day phrase their announcement.

The fine old crusted flavour that hangs round the contest still is not merely owing to the fact that ever since 1791 the name of the happy winner has been preserved, a record much older than either the Wingfield Sculls or the Professional Championship, but also to the happy circumstance of the ancient and hospitable patronage under which the race is rowed. The old hall of the famous Fishmongers' Company [1] perished in the great Fire, and, on a site which was worth over half a million an acre even seventy years ago, the third edifice was rebuilt by Roberts in 1830, on that new London Bridge which was opened by William IV and Queen Adelaide in 1831, on that very first of August consecrated by Doggett " for ever " to the race that still starts from these historic arches. The statue of Sir William Walworth, holding in his hand

---

[1] The History of the Fishmongers' Company has been so fully written elsewhere by better pens than mine, that I need say very little here of the records that go back at least as far as the charter of Edward III. A short but very valuable illustrated account of the portraits, pictures, and plate possessed by the Company has just been published by Mr. J. Wrench Towse, Clerk of the Company, to whom I am indebted for much assistance and information. I have seen in Mr. A. M. Broadley's collection the original charter of admission to the Company of H.R.H. the Duke of Sussex (whose picture by Beechey is in the Hall) signed by John David Towse, on May 23, 1816. The portraits of this John David Towse and his son, William Beckwith Towse, are in the Hall of the Company which their descendant serves so faithfully to-day. Here also are many relics of direct interest to the present purpose of these pages ; among them a chair, with a seat made from part of the foundation-stone of Old London

The Old Swan, Chelsea, in 1869.

a representation of the weapon by which Wat Tyler fell,[1] is on the
great staircase, as a reminder that fifty Lord Mayors have been
supplied by the Company to the City Government.

Among its other cherished relics is a chair made from wood
and stone brought up in 1832 from the foundations of Old London
Bridge, which were put down in June 1176 by Peter of Colechurch.
The long interval is almost covered by the history of the Company
which guards these historic remnants, for the Fishmongers were
a guild more than seven hundred years ago, and by letters patent
in 1364 were incorporated into a " Mistery." One of their most
famous pageants in those early days was the welcome to King
Edward I on his return from his Scottish victories, in which gilded
sturgeon, silver salmon, and a thousand horsemen bore a glorious
part. To the third Edward they gave a sum of money towards
the French wars which was the second largest subscription in London.
The seventh Edward himself enjoys the privileges of the Company,
in which his father and his grandfather before him had been also
freemen.

It is under such excellent auspices as these that the race takes
place every year, and I wish I were able in this place to give some
faint adumbration of its varied interest ; of the crowd of tugs and
steamers bellowing encouragement to the champions of Bermondsey, of Twickenham, of Greenwich, or of Chelsea, each boy in his
distinctive colours ; of the skill and hazards of the contest, as a
string of barges, or an indignant tug, comes tearing down to the
Pool from Putney right across the course ; of the hair-breadth escape

Bridge, and its frame-work fashioned from part of the original piles. On a plate at
the back is the following inscription :—

" This chair was made by J. Ovenston, 72 Great Titchfield Street, London,
from a design given by the Rev. W. Joliffe, Curate of Colmar in Hampshire, and
made entirely from the wood and stone taken up from the foundation of Old
London Bridge in July 1832, having remained there 656 years, being put down
in June, 1176, by the builder, Peter, a priest who was vicar of Colechurch. And
'tis rather curious that a priest should begin the bridge and after so long a period
that a parson should clear it entirely away."

In the Company's Hall are also some fine water-colour paintings of London Bridge
at various ages, by Yates ; of Waterford Ferry in 1787, by J. T. Serres ; and of the
fire at Old London Bridge in 1758, by Wright of Derby.

[1] The actual dagger is preserved in a glass case.

LONDON BRIDGE IN 1745.
From the painting by S. Scott.

of scullers in their dancing cockle-shells of cedar and of canvas; of the winning post and its flag resplendent with the crowned fishes of the Company; and of the return in the quiet murmur of a splendid sunset to the basement of that great hall close to the spot where the old Wine-Shades stood when Doggett was alive. You can almost hear, in the twilight, the silvery laugh of Bracegirdle as she trips ashore, with a jest of Congreve's own, or Steele's, that makes the very ghost of Thomas Doggett chuckle.

By how slight an occurrence may man's memory be fixed in the hearts of posterity! Alas, poor Doggett! "Where be your gibes now, your gambols, your songs, your flashes of merriment that were wont to set the table on a roar? Not one now to mock your own grinning? Quite chopfallen?" I can end no better than by quoting those lines, written only sixteen years after his death on a window-pane at Lambeth, by some young sculler, belike, with more of muscle than of metre in his composition:—

> Tom Doggett, the greatest sly droll in his parts,
> In Acting was certain a master of arts;
> A monument left—no herald is fuller—
> His praise is sung yearly by many a sculler.
> Ten thousand years hence, if the world last so long,
> Tom Doggett will still be the theme of their song.
> When Old Noll with Lewis and Bourbon are forgot,
> And when numberless Kings in oblivion shall rot.

I now leave to Mr. Nickalls the congenial task of sketching the history of the sculling-race itself; and for the remaining pages Mr. Nickalls is alone responsible. It will be a fitting introduction to them if I add here a few references to the race extracted for me from the Company's Records by the kindness of Mr. Towse. They are as follows:—

Court, Oct. 6, 1721 . . .	Company asked to accept £300 Trust.
Court, Nov. 29, 1721 . . .	Company accepted and agreed to add £50, deeds to be drawn up.
Court, July 3, 1723 . . .	Four Members appointed to see to Race and 2 guineas allowed for expenses.
Court, Aug. 1, 1760 . . .	Clerk to Watermen's Company presented Rules for Race—referred to a Committee which met September 16, 1760, and drew up regulations.
Court, June 21, 1784 . . .	Jas. Bowler declared to be Winner and to have Coat and Badge for 1783.

Court, Oct. 27, 1801 . . . . Apology inserted in papers by Competitors.

Feb. 11, 1808 . . . . . £200 South Sea Stock in name of Company—under codicil of will of Sir Wm. Jolliffe interest to be applied ⅝ to second and ⅜ to third.

July 12, 1849 . . . . . Notice of Motion by Prime Warden that some additional prizes be granted.

Aug. 1848 . . . . . . John Fry came in second but was declared not to be entitled to prize owing to his having got out of his boat for water to be baled out.

Aug. 1, 1849 . . . . . Court agreed to give £1 1s. to 1st, £1 11s. 6d. to 4th and £1 1s. each to 5th and 6th.

Aug. 1, 1861 . . . . . Frank Towers of the Victoria Theatre gave winner £3 3s. and £1 1s. each to 2nd and 3rd.

Aug. 1, 1864 . . . . . Jas. Weston and J. C. Selwyn, Q.C., M.P. Chairman of the Thames Regatta proposed sundry alterations, including a suggestion that the Race should be rowed with the tide and the distance shortened.

Sept. 30, 1869 . . . . . Gift to Winner increased from 1 to 5 guineas.

Aug. 1, 1872 . . . . . Prizes to 4th, 5th and 6th increased to £2 2s., £1 11s. 6d. and £1 6s. respectively.

Aug. 1, 1873 . . . . . In description of Race in Court Books instead of to the Old Swan, Chelsea this year it reads—"*opposite to* the site where the Old Swan, Chelsea, *formerly stood.*"

July 14, 1887 . . . . . Prizes increased—

Winner	£10
Second	6
Third	5
Fourth	4
Fifth	3
Sixth	2

Dec. 17, 1903 . . . . . Court agreed to purchase for 30s. limit poetry and picture of Happy or Natty Jerry—published in 1794, and who described himself as winner of Doggett's prize. He afterwards went to sea.

Feb. 14, 1907. . . . . . Court agreed to remove "all restrictions as to style and build of boat."

Part II

THE RACE

BY GUY NICKALLS

WATERMAN'S TICKET.

CHAPTER VIII

Thames Watermen

Our gains will scarce afford a draught
Of liquor down our throat;
And neither we, nor yet our craft,
Can keep ourselves afloat.

IN the dim prehistoric ages we have every reason to believe that the ancient Briton paddled about on the River Thames in his dug-out, and no doubt used it as a highway to move east or west as hunger or his enemies compelled. The very earliest authentic records we have of toll-taking occurred somewhere about the year 850 A.D., when the Vikings, during one of their raids on England, sailed and rowed up the river as far as Taplow, where, losing a chief, they buried him with some pomp and circumstance in the grounds now occupied by an even greater chief, viz. Lord Desborough, who, in the person of Chairman of the Thames Conservancy, now rules over the destinies of the river from Teddington Lock upwards. The tolls not voluntarily paid had been extracted by force since early days from the rich Thanes and the richer monastic orders who lived on its banks ; and after a time, when the Thames became the King's highway and the only safe and passable highway in the kingdom, it became a matter of bargaining and wrangling with the boat owner if one wished to be rowed up, down, or across the river.

To avoid this, and for the protection of the public, a list of legal fares was drawn up ; and finally King Henry VIII of immortal memory, in the sixth year of his reign (1514), passed a statute for regulating watermen and their fares, recording : " That it had been a laudable custome and usage tyme out of mind to use the river in Barge or Whery Bote," and thus founded the " Watermen's Company," which has proved of inestimable benefit to the waterside population for nearly four hundred years.

It is not my intention to write again what has already been well done, namely a history of the Watermen's Company; but a book on the race for Doggett's Coat and Badge would not be considered complete without some mention, however cursory, of the Company who bound apprentices and issued licences to the watermen who competed in the race.

From the early days when the Barons arrived at Runnymede Island in their state barges to force King John sign the Magna Charta, down to the middle of the eighteenth century, the river, as has been said, was the best means of conveyance both for royalty and the public between the Tower, Windsor, Westminster, Greenwich, Whitehall, Sheen, Hampton, Bridewell, etc.; and it therefore became the duty of the Watermen's Company to draw up a scale of legal fares; to control in every manner the men who plied for hire on the river; to apprentice them; to see that they were capable of handling boats with safety to the passengers when they took up their freedom; to arm them, to ensure that their passengers were not murdered, assaulted or robbed; to issue licences to lightermen; to renew licences triennially to freemen; and generally to act the shepherd over a somewhat turbulent flock. In olden days they also issued lists of public plying places for watermen above and below bridge, which later they marked with a broad arrow and date thus: ⬆. I have printed below one of their
1814
lists issued in 1708. They also received the orders of the Lord High Admiral, and carried them into effect, with regard to the impressment of watermen for the Navy.

I will refer to their more modern duties and responsibilities later on; for the present I need only add that they fulfilled in a most adequate manner their various and multitudinous offices; in former times their Court sat to settle disputes, and though they had no power of enforcing their judgment except the cancelling of licences, their verdicts were very seldom appealed against.

FLAG OF THE WATERMEN'S COMPANY.

In Pepys' time we know that round and about London there were some 10,000 licensed watermen besides a few hundred lightermen. The percentage has exactly altered now, for out of 5,240 licensed lightermen and watermen only some 260 are watermen; and the number of apprentices has in a like manner fallen off, for where there were some 4,000 or 5,000 there are to-day only 1272. Unfortunately for us the Great Fire of 1666 destroyed the Watermen's Hall, and all its records and much interesting detail has been lost. There was a list of fares published in 1559, which was revised in 1671 (the original perished in the fire). It was again remade in 1708. Some more attempts at revision took place in 1737 and 1751. There were reprints in 1742 and again in 1770. The short list for 1671 and the longer list of 1770 were as follows :—

The fixing of the Rates or Fares of Watermen by Antient Act of Parliament is in yᵉ Power of the Lord Mayor and Court of Aldermen by whom thev were last set forth September 7, 1671, and are as follows :—

	Oars.	Sculls.
	s. d.	s. d.
Over the water directly	0 4	0 2
From London Bridge to Westminster Stairs or from any one of the Stairs to another between the Bridge and Westminster Stairs	0 6	0 3
From any of yᵉ Stairs above Bridge and below Pauls Wharf to Lambeth and Vaux Hall	1 0	0 6
From Pauls Wharf, Black Fryers, Dorset or Temple Stairs, etc. to Lambeth and Vaux Hall	0 8	0 4
From White Hall to Lambeth or Vaux Hall	0 6	0 3

Note yᵉ Fares are yᵉ same on either side yᵉ river.

1770

A table of the rates or prices appointed by the Lord Mayor and Court of Aldermen of the City of London, to be taken by the watermen rowing from place to place upon the river of Thames between Gravesend and Windsor.

From London to Gravesend, one whole fare, in oars 4s. 6d., with company 9d.
From London to Grays, one whole fare, in oars 4s., with company 8d.
From London to Greenhithe, one whole fare, in oars 4s., with company 8d.
From London to Purfleet or Erith, one whole fare, in oars 3s., with company 6d.
From London to Woolwich, one whole fare, in oars 2s. 6d., with company 4d.
From London to Blackwall, one whole fare, in oars 1s. 6d., with company 3d.
From London to Greenwich, one whole fare, in oars 1s. 6d., with company 3d.
From London to Deptford, one whole fare in oars 1s. 6d., with company 3d.
From London to Limehouse, one whole fare in oars 1s., a sculler's fare 6d.
From London to New Crane, Shadwell Dock, Bell Wharf, Ratcliffe Cross, one oar's fare 1s., a sculler 3d.

From London to Wapping Dock, Wapping News, Wapping Old Stairs, one oar's
fare 6*d.*, a sculler 3*d.*

From London to the Hermitage in oars 6*d.*, a sculler 3*d.*

From London to Rotherhithe Church Stairs and Rotherhithe Stairs, in oars
6*d.*, a sculler 3*d.*

From St. Olaves to Rotherhithe Church Stairs and Rotherhithe Stairs, in oars
6*d.*, a sculler 3*d.*

From Billingsgate or St. Olave's to St. Saviour's Mill, in oars 6*d.*, a sculler 3*d.*

Over the water directly, between London Bridge and Limehouse, for the next
sculler 2*d.*

All the stairs between London Bridge and Westminster, in oars 6*d.*, a sculler 3*d.*

From London Bridge either side, above the said bridge to Lambeth and Vauxhall,
in oars 1*s.*, a sculler 6*d.*

From Whitehall to Lambeth and Vauxhall, in oars 6*d.*, a sculler 3*d.*

From Temple Stairs, Dorset Stairs, Blackfriars, Pauls Wharf to Lambeth, in
oars 8*d.*, a sculler 2*d.*

Over the water directly, in the next boat, between London Bridge and Vauxhall,
in a sculler 2*d.*

From London to Chelsea, Battersea and Wandsworth, one whole fare, in oars
1*s.* 6*d.*, with company 3*d.*

From London to Putney, Fulham, Barn Elms, one whole fare, in oars 2*s.*, with
company 4*d.*

From London to Hammersmith, Chiswick and Mortlake, one whole fare, in oars
2*s.* 6*d.*, with company 3*d.*

From London to Brentford, Iselworth, Richmond, one whole fare in oars 3*s.* 6*d.*,
with company 6*d.*

From London to Twickenham, one whole fare, in oars 4*s.*, with company 6*d.*

From London to Kingston, one whole fare, in oars 5*s.*, with company 9*d.*

From London to Hampton Court, one whole fare, in oars 6*s.*, with company 1*s.*

From London to Hampton Town, Sunbury and Walton upon Thames, one
whole fare, in oars 7*s.*, with company 1*s.*

From London to Weybridge and Chertsey, one whole fare, in oars 10*s.*, with
company 1*s.*

From London to Staines, one whole fare, in oars 12., with company 1*s.*

From London to Windsor, one whole fare, in oars 14*s.*, with company 2*s.*

The following rate of charges for crossing at the Horse Ferry
at Westminster is the only record I have found :—

	s.	d.		s.	d.
Man and Horse	0	2	Coach and Six Horses	2	6
Horse and Chaze	1	0	Cart Laden	2	6
Coach and two Horses	1	6	A Cart or Waggon each	2	0
Coach and Four Horses	2	0			

Proprietor, Mr. Cole and two or three others.

Modern fares are heavier ; take for instance London Bridge

to Wapping Stairs, the ancient fare was 6d. and 3d., the moderne fare is 1s. 6d. and 9d.

From London Bridge to Chelsea used to be 1s. 6d. and 3d., but is now 5s. and 2s. 6d.

From London Bridge to Deptford was 1s. 6d. and 3d., and now is 4s. 6d. and 2s. 3d.

From London Bridge to Greenwich was 1s. 6d. and 3d., and is now 5s. and 2s. 6d.

From London Bridge to Limehouse was 1s. and 6d., and to-day is 3s. and 1s. 6d.

Again in olden days one could get rowed from London Bridge to Windsor for 14s. I think it would be hard to-day to find a man willing to do it for the same fee.

Now the watermen who took these fees and plied at these Stairs appeared to have differed very little from their more modern prototypes who ply at Limehouse Ferry to-day, except perhaps in language. The old-time ferryman was disgustingly coarse, not to the point, and very long-winded. The language of the modern bargee is, one might almost say, concise, pointed, fervent, and of a rosy hue. Let us see how he is described in Ned Warde's *London Spy*; it is thus : " A Jolly Grizzle Pated Charon handed us into his Wherry, whips off his short skirted doublet whereon was a badge to show whose fool he was, then fixes his stretcher, bids us trim the boat and away he rowed us, but we had not swum above the length of a West country barge before a scoundrel crew of Lambeth Gardeners attacked us with such a volley of fancy nonsense that it made my eyes stare, my head ake, my tongue run and my ears tingle, one of them beginning with us in this manner . . ." There then follows a page of the most lurid language imaginable.

These watermen, as has been said, led an extremely hard life of it, especially, as was often the case, when the Thames was frozen over and they could take no fares. They were also impressed very severely for the Navy, and there was therefore often a dearth of them, as Pepys mentions ; and to escape impressment the lightermen coming down river used to get off at Kingston and disappear after receiving their wages, leaving the lighters to be taken to London by old and decrepit men who were of no use to the press gang. It was for young men of this class who had just got free of their apprenticeship that Doggett catered when he left funds to provide a Coat and Badge to be annually rowed for. The pity of it is that their quaint and picturesque uniforms have disappeared. Watermen were the first public servants who ever wore a uniform. Long before our Army and Navy adopted any distinguishing garb, Thames watermen were known by their uniform and badge, a pleated coat, knee breeches and stockings, and hat according to fashion, but always a plate on the arm, either of the Watermen's Hall to denote that they had the freedom of the river and were licensed, or the badge of their employer. Any person rowing or working any boat, wherry, or other vessel, who had not served seven years as apprentice, incurred a penalty of £10.

The places at which licensed watermen might ply were as under :—

ABOVE BRIDGE

North Side.	*South Side.*
Old Swan.	Pepper Alley.
Cole Harbour.	
Steele Yard Stairs.	St. Saviour's.
1. Dowgate. 2. Three Grain Stairs.	1. Bank End. 2. Horshoe Ally.
Queen Hithe.	New Thames Street.
Trig Stairs.	Montstrand Street.
Paul's Wharf.	Falcon Stairs.
Common Stairs *or*	
Puddle Dock.	Paris Garden Lane.
Black Fryers.	Marygold Stairs.
Dorset Stairs.	Bull Stairs.
White Fryers.	Old Barge House.
Temple Stairs.	
Essex Stairs.	Morriss' Causeway.
Arundle Stairs.	
Surrey Stairs.	
Strand Stairs.	Cupid's or Cuper's Stairs.
Somerset Stairs	
Savoy Stairs.	
Worcester Stairs.	
Salisbury Stairs.	
Ivy Stairs Bridge.	
Exchange Stairs.	King's Arms Stairs.

ABOVE BRIDGE

North Side.	*South Side.*
York Stairs.	
Black Lyon Stairs.	
Hungerford.	
Whitehall Stairs.	
Priory Garden.	
Manchester Stairs.	
Westminster Bridge.	Standgate Stairs.
Parliament Stairs.	
Horseferry, Westminster.	⎧ Horseferry, Lambeth
	⎨ White Hart
	⎩ Vauxhall

BELOW BRIDGE

North Side.	*South Side.*
Billingsgate Stairs.	Tooley Street.
Sabb's Stairs.	
Custom House.	Battle Bridge.
Tower Dock.	Pickle Herring.
Irongate Stairs.	Still Stairs.
St. Katherine Stairs.	Old Stairs.
	New Stairs.
Ship Brewhouse.	Savory's Mill Stairs.
Hermitage Stairs.	East Lane Stairs.
Wapping Old Stairs.	Three Mariners Stairs.
Wapping New Stairs.	Fountain Stairs.
	Mill Stairs.
Execution Dock.	Rotherhithe or Rederiff Stairs.
Wapping Dock.	King Stairs.
King Edward Stairs.	Elephant Stairs.
	Church Stairs.
New Crane.	Swan Stairs.
King James' Stairs.	
Shadwell Stairs.	
Bell Wharf.	Globe Stairs.
Ratcliff Cross.	
Kidney Stairs at Limehouse Bridge.	Shepherd and Dog Stairs.
Duke Shore.	Pageant Stairs.

It may be added that the cost of taking barges up the river was also heavy in the eighteenth century. For in the *Ambulator*, 1774, we read that " the navigation of the river is attended with considerable expense, for a barge passing from Lechlade to London pays for passing through the locks £13 15*s.* 6*d.*, and from Oxford

to London £12 18s. This charge is, however, only a summer one
when the water is low; and there is no lock on the river from
London Bridge to Bolters Lock, that is for the space of fifty-one
miles and a half above bridge."

The Watermen's Company still binds apprentices, mostly for
five years now, and grants freedoms to contestants for Doggett's
Coat and Badge as it did 190 years ago. An equally important
part of the duty of the Company is the measurement of all barges
on the river, these craft alone numbering some 10,000. It is also
responsible for the measurement of all pleasure craft let out to
the public below Teddington Lock; these boats number between
two and three thousand. The authority to measure these boats
was obtained by the Company in an Act passed at great cost to
the Company in 1893, which has proved a strong protection to
the public, the number of lives lost through overcrowding since
that date having been reduced to a minimum. The Company
was the first river authority in the Kingdom to seek for and obtain
this power, and the Thames Conservancy do not even at this date
exercise similar jurisdiction above Teddington Lock.

The boats used for Doggett's race have changed from heavy
lumbering craft to perfect models of lightness and elegance, weighing some 25 lb. The course, although the same in distance, and
starting and finishing at the same old places, or rather the spots
where those old taverns the "Old Swan" and the "White Swan"
used to be, differs in that now the race is rowed up with the
strongest of the tide, instead of at the time when the tide was
worst against them; it consequently is now rowed in quicker time
by about an hour.

The Fishmongers' Company still govern and arrange the race,
although their method of obtaining the six competitors differs
from the old method, in that all entrants are allowed to compete
in trial races or heats, which are now rowed from Putney to
Hammersmith three weeks or so before the race, and they are no
longer chosen by lot. Instead of wherries, galley boats, etc.,
following the race, we nowadays have a small crowd of steamers
and steam launches each cheering on its own favourite. And

lastly, no mistakes are made nowadays as regards the name of the winner, but careful records are kept of it.

We might remind our readers also that if the present Government has its way and passes the Port of London Bill, the Watermen's Company, the system of apprenticeship, and the whole thing will be ended. No more races for Doggett's Coat and Badge can be held under the conditions prevailing at present. Then indeed could we say with Dibdin :—

> Then farewell, my trim-built wherry,
> Oars and boat and Badge farewell ;
> Nevermore at Chelsea Ferry
> Shall your Thomas take a spell.

CHAPTER IX

Some Famous Watermen, 1700-1800

A plague on all reforming chaps—
I vishes they were dead;
And then a vaterman, perhaps,
Might arn a bit of bread.

IN 1730 a very celebrated waterman named John Reeves, who plied at Essex Stairs, died. He got a comfortable living by attending anglers with his boat. His hire was 2s. a day, and a certain number of persons, who were accustomed thus to employ him, raised a sum sufficient to buy him a waterman's coat and silver badge, the impress whereof was " himself with an angler in his boat." And he had annually a new coat to the time of his death.

There were quantities of roach, dace, perch, plaice, smelts, flounders, salmon, shad, eels, gudgeon, dabs, etc., and at that day salmon were so plentiful that on June 7, 1749, two great draughts were caught in nets, thirty-five large salmon in one and twenty-two in the other. There is a fishing tackle shop in Crooked Lane near London Bridge, a relic of the days when fish were more plentiful at London Bridge than they are to-day, and the local angler had to be catered for as regards tackle and bait. In fact I am told that all the tackle shops in proximity to London Bridge had their origin in those days.

On July 24, 1797, Lord Nelson attempted to take Santa Cruz in the Island of Teneriffe, when he lost his right arm, the same shot killing Samuel Shillingford, his favourite coxswain. Shillingford was a waterman of Greenwich, bound apprentice in 1786, made free in 1792, who was afterwards with many others summoned and drafted into the Royal Navy from Watermen's Hall.

In 1758 the Government were in great want of seamen to man the fleet for the anticipated war with Spain ; and on July 25 the Watermen's Company were commanded to raise three thousand sailors for the ships of war fitting out, and impress warrants were granted for the purpose. On the Wednesday and Thursday following fifteen hundred men were impressed, and on August 2 two large birds having settled on St. Paul's Church caused a great crowd to assemble. This led to the following expedient being resorted to. The press gang on August 5 placed a live turkey on the top of the Monument which in a short time drawing together a great number of idle persons, they had the opportunity of selecting such a number of men as answered the purpose of their intended scheme.

Royalty and private individuals kept their watermen in the old days, as they keep their chauffeurs now. These men were given a livery, i.e. a waterman's coat and a silver badge with the crest or sign of their employer on it, and all men of importance had their watermen. Pepys mentions several of his by name. The large City companies also employed great numbers, as all pageants in those days took place in their barges on the river, some of which still exist. One of the watermen's songs, preserved by the Fishmongers' Company, was :—

> I was the pride of the Thames,
>   My name was Natty Jerry,
> The best of Smart and flashy dames,
>   I've carried in my Wherry.
>
> For then no mortal soul like me,
>   So merrily did jog it,
> I lov'd my wife, my friend, d'ye see,
>   And won the prize of Doggett.
>
> In Coat and Badge so neat and spruce,
>   I row'd all blithe and merry,
> And every Waterman did use
>   To call me Happy Jerry.

The songs of " Poor Jack," " The Jolly Waterman," " Tom Bowling," " Ben Bolt," " Tom Tough," etc., were written by Charles Dibdin, of world-wide celebrity. He wrote about fourteen hundred of them, and his patriotic songs in particular were very popular; and the Government requirements for the Navy being great, he was employed by them to write, sing, and give away war songs for the purpose of influencing watermen and others to join the Navy, for which he afterwards received a pension of £200 per annum. He died in 1804. These said watermen were a hardy lot and often lived to a ripe old age, as we find in 1774 that Evan Lindsay, a waterman of Rotherhithe, who had worked on the river upwards of eighty years, was at last found dead in his boat. His age was ninety-eight.

In 1777 a remarkable trial of a waterman named Holderness took place. It appears that some gentlemen stepped on board his wherry and demanded to be taken down river. He refused and a quarrel ensued, during which the waterman foundered his boat in 14 feet of water. No lives were lost, but complaint was made to the Watermen's Company, who held that no sculler was obliged by law to go further down than Cuckolds Point, nor further up than Vauxhall. The gentlemen should have engaged oars, and that above and below these places there were no settled fares. On the case being taken to the Sessions the waterman was convicted, but on the intercession of the prosecutors, was let off with three months' imprisonment. Evidently there was a radius corresponding more or less to our present cab radius, beyond which a passenger could not compel his boatmen to take him, but the extreme measure of upsetting his cab would scarcely be resorted to by the modern Jehu when asked to take a fare beyond his radius.

Of a very large collection of prints of watermen, very kindly lent to me by my friend Mr. A. M. Broadley, I have chosen one for reproduction here which shows us the waterman of ancient times at his best.

From a newspaper of 1734 I extract the following :—

> Last Saturday the noted Stephens, a Waterman of White-friars, and Richard Graham, alias Oliver Bumble, rowed for ten Guineas from the Old Swan to the Swan at Chelsea, which was won with Difficulty by the former. There was about £300 depending.

Have times altered one whit ? are not watermen of to-day

the same as of yore ? Have we not our "Doggett Cobbs," our
"Bossy Phelps," our "Goosey Drivers," etc. ? A curious riverside custom this, of nicknames, or rather prenomens. In a little
book entitled a *Book for a Rainy Day* we find that there was a
portion of the burial ground of St. Martin's in the Fields at
Charing Cross set apart especially for the burial of Thames watermen, and the author mentions one " Copper Holmes," his waterman, who was buried there. There is no doubt where he got his
prenomen. Driver tells me he got his from the extraordinarily
clever way in which he as a boy imitated the noise a goose makes.
His friends used to say : " Here's a penny, show us how you can
copy a goose." Cobb got his nickname of Doggett, I am told,
because after winning the great event he could talk of nothing
else. I can hardly believe this though, knowing him as I do, and
if this is a libel or slander, I must apologize in advance. He is a
well-known riverside character, and I, for one, regret that his son
did not follow in his father's footsteps last year.

Thanks to his kindness, however, I am enabled to give the
wording of an exemption pass carried by watermen of people of
any importance, which prevented them being seized by the press
gang for the Navy. This particular pass belonged to his great-
grandfather, who was waterman to the Earl of Thanet, and reads
thus :—

> Whereas I the Earl of Thanet have appointed the Bearer Richard Cobb to
> be one of my watermen to give Personal attendance on me, these are therefore
> to will and request you to permission my said servant to pass and repass on his
> and my occasion and his will and pleasure without any of your Imprests or Molesta-
> tion whatsoever, which may anywise tend to the hindrance of mine or his business
> without leave first had from me, and you will answer the contrary at your peril.
> Given under my hand and seal of arms. This twenty first day of April in the
> thirty first year of the reign of our Sovereign Lord King George third in the year
> of Our Lord One thousand seven hundred and ninety one.
>
> To all His Majesty's Officers Military and Civil Impress Masters or whom-
> soever this may concern.
>
> "THANET" (Seal)

From the look of this piece of parchment it seems that Mr.
Richard Cobb had more than once been over-board, as it shows

signs of being soaked through, and in several places the writing is consequently almost illegible.

They were grand material for the Navy, and the press gang knew it, so there was always an eager rush to try and obtain exemption passes.

These watermen, it appears, were frequently petitioning Parliament, at one time to prevent the play-actors migrating from Bankside into the City, as thereby they would lose an enormous number of ferrying fees ; at another time they petitioned Parliament to try and prevent bridges being built, as of course every bridge built meant less work for them.

CHAPTER X

History of Doggett's Race

Some say we are a worthless set,
    As obstinate as dull,
Because, as how, we cannot get
    A living by our Scull.

"MAY 18th. Towards Westminster, from the Towre by water, and was fain to stand upon one of the piers about the Bridge before the men could drag their boats through the lock, and which they could not do till another was called up to help them. Being through the Bridge I found the Thames full of boats and gallys and upon enquiry found that there was a wager to be run this morning. So spying of Payne in a gally I went with him and there staid, thinking to have gone to Chelsy with them. But upon the start the wager boats fell foul one of another, till at last one of them gives over, pretending foul play and so the other row away alone and all our sport lost."

From the above extract from *Pepys' Diary* for 1661 one can draw a fairly safe conclusion that wager races among the Thames-side watermen were of common, even if not of regular, annual occurrence long before our friend Thomas Doggett was born. The race here mentioned was evidently rowed against the tide from the Old Swan at London Bridge to the White Swan at Chelsea. Pepys mentions Chelsy as a matter of course as the finishing point, and states that but for the fouling at the start he would have got his waterman Payne to row him to the finish to see the race ; and as the Thames was full of boats and galleys all bent on the same object of taking spectators to see this wager, we may infer that then, as now, such matches created very great interest, and that 250 years of civilization have in no wise altered human nature; for people still turn up in thousands and even tens of thousands to witness any honest contest of pace, pluck and endurance on the old river Thames.

The watermen of the river were in those days as necessary as the cabmen of to-day and a very large factor in the everyday life of London. We learn from the diarist quoted above that there were from nine to ten thousand of them, and they had certain rights and privileges which they stuck to tenaciously; they also became quite a political factor to be reckoned with, and were not therefore to be neglected; owing, however, to the raids of the press gang for naval purposes there was often a great shortage of them at the various stairs, and getting about from place to place in London became a matter of great difficulty, the river being at that time and for a long time after, the most popular, cheapest and easiest method of transit.

The Swan Tavern at London Bridge became the recognized starting place of all such races, as Pepys describes; for not only was London Bridge the only one, and therefore a good landmark, so to speak, for these events, but races were always in those days rowed against the tide, and, as we have seen, they could not have started below bridge because of the very great difficulty of forcing a passage up the rapids which rushed through the arches, which, with their piers, blocked the river to such a degree that, when the tide ran out, dangerous eddies were at once formed. The Swan Tavern, London Bridge, was a favourite haunt of Mr. Thomas Doggett, and he had probably watched many a wherry race start from the parlour window overhanging the river; in fact, the story goes that Mr. Doggett, being at one of the stairs, wished to hire a waterman to row him up the river home, but it being a bad night and against tide the men delayed doing so. A young waterman at length offered his services, and after the journey Mr. Doggett found on inquiry that the youth had only just got his freedom of the Company and was very deserving of support; he therefore well rewarded him for his trouble, and established this match, it being the means also of commemorating the accession of the House of Hanover to the throne of England. True as this may be, it would not conflict with the theory that Mr. Thomas Doggett was merely continuing an annual race among the watermen, and by his legacy of a coat and badge was trying to ensure that the race should be rowed annually " for ever."

The river in those days was far different from the muddy murky stream we see to-day. The tide was not so confined as it is to-day and ebbed and flowed more slowly. London Bridge was the only one which spanned it in the environs of London, that and the Horseferry and Westminster being the only means of travelling south into Surrey and Kent. Salmon ran freely up to Boulters, the first lock, and the beat of oars took the place of the petrol and steam-driven screws.

From an entry in the history of the Watermen's Company in 1715, I quote the following :—

> On the first of August Thomas Doggett, comedian, a great Whig in politics, then lately joint Manager of Drury Lane Theatre with Wilks and Cibber, gave a Coat and Badge to be rowed for by six Watermen in the first year of their freedom ; it was rowed for on this day being the first anniversary of the accession of King George the First. . . .
> The Match seems to have been continued annually during his life ; he died on 22nd of September, 1721 endeared to Whigs and Watermen and was buried in the Churchyard of St. John the Evangelist, Eltham, Kent, having by his Will dated the 10th of September, 1721 hereinafter referred to, provided for the perpetual continuance of the Match. The Garrick Club possesses an original portrait of him.

His executors were Sir George Markham and Thomas Reynolds, and instructions were left to them that they should, out of his personal estate, purchase freehold lands of inheritance to the value of ten pounds per annum, and cause such lands when purchased to be conveyed to Edward Burt of the Admiralty Office, Esquire, his heirs and assigns, subject to and for ever chargeable with the laying out, furnishing and procuring yearly, on the first day of August (unless the same happen to be on a Sunday and then to be on the Monday following) for ever the following particulars, that is to say : Five pounds for a Badge of Silver weighing about twelve ounces and representing Liberty, to be rowed for by six young watermen according to his custom. Eighteen shillings for cloth for a livery whereon the said Badge is to be put ; one and twenty shillings for making up the said livery, buttons and appurtenances to it, and thirty shillings to the clerk of the Watermen's Hall (this is continued to this day). By deed dated November 29 it was agreed by his executors and the said Edward Burt that they should pay to the Fishmongers' Company the sum of £350 in discharge of such trusts, the said Company granting an annuity or rent of £10 per annum and covenanting to carry out the trusts of the said Will. By said deed it is provided that the said Badge shall also have the impress of a wild horse in such a manner as was used by Mr. Dogget in his lifetime, and round the plate there shall be in fair letters "The gift of Mr. Thomas Dogget the late famous Comedian."

As regards the other prizes in Doggett's race, in 1861, the second and third prizes were respectively five-eighths and three-eighths of the interest of £260 17s. 3d., formerly £200 worth of South Sea Stock left in the Will of Sir William Joliffe in 1820, the amounts being £4 17s. 9d. and £2 18s. 9d. The fourth prize of £1 11s. 6d. and the fifth and sixth of £1 1s. each are the gift of the Fishmongers' Company.

These are all altered now and the prize list reads as follows :—

To the 1st man £10 by the Company in addition to the Coat and Badge under Mr. Dogget's Will.

To the 2nd man £6 ⎱
 ,, ,, 3rd ,, £5 ⎰ including Sir William Jolliffe's gift of £7 3s. 4d.
 ,, ,, 4th ,, — ⎫
 ,, ,, 5th ,, — ⎬ The Company's Gifts,
 ,, ,, 6th ,, — ⎭

provided they run the entire distance and subject to the conditions enforced in former years.

So much for the actual Coat and Badge and other prizes ; a short description of the course and conditions of sculling will now follow.

The old rule was that the claimants should start off upon a given signal at the time of the tide when the current is strongest against them, from the Old Swan at London Bridge to the White Swan at Chelsea, a course of nearly five miles. In 1769 fresh articles were drawn up to prevent abuses. Boats had to be passed by the Fishmongers' Company, and six men were drawn by lot out of all the entries to compete, so that it must have very frequently happened that the best men never started at all, especially when in some years the number of entries was so large.

In 1873, I believe at the suggestion of the late Mr. Frank Playford, the six were chosen by preliminary heats, which were rowed at Putney, and it was also at his suggestion that the race was thenceforth rowed with and not against the tide. This I consider a mistake, and as regards this and the wording on the Badge, I think the conditions of the Will should be more strictly fulfilled.

Mr. Doggett once went down to see his wager rowed for, and herewith is his description of what happened :—

As I was making my way through the 'Friars intending to take water at Temple Stairs, in order that I might witness the race for my Coat and Badge, one of those rake helly fellows that so beset the town, stopped me, and cocking his hat with arms akimbo cried " Whig or Tory ? " He did not care a Queen Anne's farthing for my politics, but made it the pretext for a quarrel. I whipped out my hanger in a trice, set my back to the wall and cried, " Hurrah for King George and long life to him," and yet I had liked to have fared scurvily, had I not bethought me that my own name for the nonce would stand me in even better stead than the King's. So when being surrounded by a host of tatterdemalions and pronounced a rat that must bleed, I said be it so my masters and though you fail in the recognition, know that I am Dogget, whereat the varlits laughed ; true, I escaped with a whole skin, but at the expense of a guinea, this is the gist on't,—so now to dinner and afterwards to the White Swan there to drink a cool tankard and shake hands with the winner.

In modern days those who drink the cool tankard are those lucky enough to be the guests of the Fishmongers' Company, and they do so not at the White Swan, Chelsea, but either in the saloon of the good ss. *Queen Elizabeth*, after the race, or in the great Hall of the Company, before it. In 1780 the White Swan at Chelsea became a brewhouse of Messrs. Watney & Elliot, now Watney, Coombe, Reid & Co., and at the present day there stands on the same site a fine private residence which is called the Swan House.

We note that the race on several occasions was rowed for more than once ; and this evidently came about because Doggett's Will had a clause that should any person make affidavit that the race had been unfairly won it should be rowed again.

The race is nowadays rowed with the tide and passes under no less than eleven bridges. Our friend Doggett would indeed be astounded could he take boat at the " Old Swan " and, following his race, take note of the various styles of engineering feats expressed in these eleven bridges of iron and stone which now exist where none existed in his day.

The modern competitor at the start goes to obtain the full force of the tide as near the centre of the river as possible, and thus passes under Cannon Street Railway Bridge and also Southwark Bridge ; he then pulls his left a bit and works slightly over to the Surrey side of the stream, and should take either the second or third span from the Surrey side in passing under Blackfriars Bridge ; keeping towards the Surrey side still, but not actually hugging the shore, he passes under Waterloo Bridge through an arch, as much on the Surrey side as the moored barges there allow him. This is usually the third or fourth arch from the Surrey shore. Racing on to Hungerford Bridge, he tries to get through the fourth span from the Surrey shore, for here he knows he will receive the full benefit of the tide again, but if he be baulked of this he goes for the third span from the same shore. The men nearly always part here. Some prefer to cling to the Surrey shore until nearly at the top end of St. Thomas' Hospital. Others make the crossing for the Middlesex shore just below Westminster Bridge, passing under the second or third arch from the Middlesex side. If they do this they pass along the terrace of the Houses of Parliament and make for the Middlesex opening through the Lambeth Suspension Bridge, where the water is usually smoother. Those who have held on to the Surrey shore genera'ly join company again with their opponents at this spot. Having passed this bridge, they should rather hug the Middlesex shore, as not only is it the nearest way home, but the tide runs pretty freely down that side past the old Westminster Horse Ferry, owned at one time by the famous Cole, forebear of no less than three winners of the Coat and Badge. And so on and up through Vauxhall Bridge, where most of the competitors take the second span from the Middlesex bank ; some knowing ones, however, often choose

the Middlesex span, arguing that what they lose in tide is made
up for by smooth water. From here they pull their left a bit
until after passing Pimlico, where they should be in the centre
of the river once more, taking number two arch from the Surrey
shore under the Grosvenor Railway Bridge, and plumb through
the centre of the Victoria Foot Bridge, and make their nearest
way to the flag boat moored off the Swan House, about a hundred
and fifty yards or so below the Albert Bridge. Having passed
this, the sculler scrambles into his friend's gig which is awaiting
him, to be taken (boat and all) to the steam launch filled with
friends, backers and supporters from the district from which he
hails, there, no doubt, " to drink a cool tankard " of foaming
ale and freely discuss the events and episodes of his long and
tiring five mile pull, and thank his stars it was not against the
tide as of yore. He passes over numerous tunnels during his
journey and under the following bridges :—

> London Bridge.
>   (Start.)
> Cannon Street Railway Bridge.
> Blackfriars   do.   do.
>   do.   Foot Bridge.
> Waterloo.
> Hungerford.
> Westminster.
> Lambeth.
> Vauxhall.
> Grosvenor Railway Bridge.
> Victoria Foot Bridge.
>   (Finish.)
> Albert Bridge.

The choice for stations and their respective colours are drawn
for in the Fishmongers' Hall on the morning of the race. The
Bargemaster of the Fishmongers' Company starts the race. There
is very little fouling, and I imagine the condition still holds good
—that if a competitor considers anything done unfair and makes
affidavit to that effect, the Fishmongers' Company would order
the race to be rowed again. The mere fact that the Clerk of the
Watermen's Hall received, and, in fact, receives to this day, a fee
of thirty shillings for the race points to the fact that at one time

David Coombes, the Celebrated Sculler,
Winner of Doggett's Coat and Badge.

the whole thing was arranged by that Company, and we have been unable to discover why Mr. Doggett in his will left it under the control of the Fishmongers' Company.

The boats used in the race now are far different from those used some two hundred years ago. Originally the men rowed in their ordinary heavy passenger wherries, strong clumsy craft capable of holding three or four passengers, and as these were rowed against the tide it is not surprising to learn that in some years the contestants took nearly two hours to get the distance. As is the way of men, they gradually began to lighten these craft as much as possible by leaving bottom boards and all unnecessary paraphernalia at home, until they gradually got to build a lighter type of craft for racing purposes altogether, so that those who could afford to do this gained a very great advantage over their poorer brethren. Abuses of this sort had to be put a stop to, with the result that in 1769 new rules and regulations were drawn up, and all boats had to be examined and passed by the Fishmongers' Company; and they took good care to see that these were proper, full-sized, licensed wherries—in fact for many years the boats were supplied by the Company and merely allotted to the contestants. The character of the craft with the abolition and disuse of wherries and ferries then began to alter quickly enough, until at last they came to rowing in boats known as "old fashion boats." These were boats with wooden wings, so to speak, as iron outriggers were not allowed; the sides of the boat were carried up and out, the boats got narrower and narrower, and the wooden wings, which of course now assumed the form of wooden outriggers, had their interstices filled in with thin cedar planking. Although best and best boats in reality, except for the open proper steel outrigger, they were used up to and including 1906, and were exceedingly hard boats to sit, as, if a wave got on top of the wing it held the boat down on one scull with no chance of recovery, or if a short sea hit it underneath it nearly rolled the man over the other way. Never shall I forget the sight of six weary men in 1906 battling against a raging sea in Westminster Reach, utterly unable now and again to scull at all, the boats full, their arms tired, missing the water mostly, or anyway stopping entirely, every few seconds, to try and bear up under the strain of a huge sea fairly smothering man and boat in mad turmoil.

This last year, very wisely on Mr. Fred Fenner's suggestion, these silly wings were allowed to disappear and the proper " best and best " boat immediately took their place. A sculler myself, I cannot understand how these men remain in their boats at all. This long course is not so much a test of speed as a test of watermanship and endurance, which after all are more the qualities required of a man who is going to get his living on the water as waterman or lighterman.

The Start of the Race.

From the Survey of London in 1745.

CHAPTER XI

List of Winners

A boat, my master, to the shores
Of Battersea or Fulham ?
And if you wish a pair of oars,
An't I the boy to pull 'em ?

1716	Edward Bishop or E. Gullyford	
1719	John Dolbey	Rotherhith.
1721	C. Gurney	Foxhall.
1722	William Morris	Rotherhith.
1723	Edward Howard	Capers or Cupids Bridge.
1726	Thomas Barrow	Sunbury.
1728	John Gibbs	St. Mary Overy.
1729	John Bean	Steel Yard.
1730	John Broughton	Hungerford.
1731	J. Aliss	Battersea.
1732	R. Adam	Masons.
1733	W. Swabby	Whitehall.
1734	J. Bellows	Black Lion.
1735	H. Watford	Temple.
1736	W. Hilliard	Westminster.
1737	J. Heaver	Battersea.
1738	J. Oakes	King's Arms.
1739	George Harrington	St. Saviours.
1740	J. Wing	Whitefryers.
1741	D. Roberts	St. Mary Overy.
1743	A. Wood	
1744	J. Polton	Marigold.

1745	J. Blasdale	
1746	J. White	
1747	J. Joyner	Beer Quay.
1748	Thomas Wagdon	Whitefryers.
1749	H. Hilden	Mills Stairs.
1750	J. Duncombe	Blackfryers.
1751	J. Earle	Irongate.
1752	J. Hogden	
1753	N. Sandford	Masons Stair.
1754	Adam Marshall	St. Saviours.
1755	C. Gill	Old Swan.
1757	John White	Putney.
1758	J. Danby	Christ Church.
1759	J. Clarke	Blackfryers.
1760	E. Wood	
1761	W. Penner	
1762	W. Wood	
1763	S. Eggleton	St. Pauls.
1764	John Morris	Horseferry.
1765	R. Eggleton	St. Catherines.
1768	W. Watson	Westminster
1770	Thomas Goddard	Greenwich.
1771	A. Badmann	Queenhithe.
1772	H. Briggs	Somerset.
1773	J. Frovley	Marigold.
1777	J. Pickering	Greenhithe.
1776	W. Price	Mills.
1778	H. J. B. Pearson	Lambeth.
1779	W. Boddington	Brickwell.
1780	J. J. Bradshaw	Pickle Herring
1781	W. Reeves	
1782	Trucke	Tower.
1783	James Bowler	
1784	John Davis	Greenhithe.
1786	J. Nash	King's Stairs Horsley-down.

1787	B. Rawlinson	.	.	.	Bankside.
1788	Thomas Radbourne		.	.	Wandsworth.
1789	J. Curtis	.	.	.	.
1790	Byers .	.	.	.	
1791	T. Easton .	.	.	.	Old Swan.
1792	J. Kettleby	.	.	.	Westminster.
1793	A. Haley	.	.	.	Horselydown.
1794	J. Franklin .	.	.	.	Putney.
1795	W. Parry	.	.	.	Hungerford.
1796	J. Thompson	.	.	.	Wapping O. Stairs.
1797	J. Hill	.	.	.	Bankside.
1798	T. Williams	.	.	.	Ratcliffe Cross.
1799	J. Dixon	.	.	.	Paddington St.
1800	J. Burgoyne	.	.	.	Blackfriars.
1801	J. Curtis	.	.	.	Queenhithe.
1802	W. Burns	.	.	.	Limehouse.
1803	J. Flower	.	.	.	Hungerford.
1804	C. Gingle	.	.	.	Temple.
1805	T. Johnson	.	.	.	Vauxhall.
1806	J. Goodwin	.	.	.	Ratcliffe Cross.
1807	J. Evans	.	.	.	Mill Stairs.
1808	G. Newell .	.	.	.	Battle-Bridge.
1809	F. Jury	.	.	.	Hermitage.
1810	J. Smart	.	.	.	Strand.
1811	W. Thornton	.	.	.	Hungerford.
1812	R. May	.	.	.	Westminster.
1813	R. Farson	.	.	.	Bankside.
1814	R. Harris	.	.	.	Bankside.
1815	J. Scott	.	.	.	Bankside.
1816	T. Senham .	.	.	.	Blackfriars.
1817	J. Robson .	.	.	.	Wapping O. Stairs.
1818	W. Nicholls	.	.	.	Greenwich.
1819	W. Emery .	.	.	.	Hungerford.
1820	J. Hartley .	.	.	.	Strand.
1821	T. Cole, Sen.	.	.	.	Chelsea.
1822	W. Noulton	.	.	.	Lambeth.

1823	G. Butcher	.	.	.	Hungerford.
1824	G. Fogo	.	.	.	Battle-Bridge.
1825	G. Staple	.	.	.	Battle-Bridge.
1826	J. Poett	.	.	.	Bankside.
1827	J. Voss	.	.	.	Fountain Stairs.
1828	R. Mallett	.	.	.	Lambeth.
1829	S. Stubbs	.	.	.	Old Barge House.
1830	W. Butler	.	.	.	Vauxhall.
1831	R. Oliver	.	.	.	Deptford.
1832	R. Waight	.	.	.	Bankside.
1833	G. Maynard	.	.	.	Lambeth.
1834	W. Tomlinson	.	.	.	Whitehall.
1835	W. Dryson	.	.	.	Kidney Stairs.
1836	J. Morris	.	.	.	Horselydown.
1837	T. Harrison	.	.	.	Bankside.
1838	S. Bridge	.	.	.	Kidney Stairs.
1839	T. Goodrum	.	.	.	Vauxhall Stair.
1840	W. Hawkins	.	.	.	Kidney Stairs.
1841	R. Moore	.	.	.	Surrey Canal.
1842	J. Liddey	.	.	.	Wandsworth.
1843	J. Fry	.	.	.	Kidney Stairs.
1844	F. Lett	.	.	.	Lambeth.
1845	F. Cobb	.	.	.	Greenwich.
1846	J. Wing	.	.	.	Pimlico.
1847	W. Ellis	.	.	.	Westminster.
1848	J. Ash	.	.	.	Rotherhithe.
1849	T. Cole, Jun.	.	.	.	Chelsea.
1850	W. Campbell	.	.	.	Westminster.
1851	G. Wigget	.	.	.	Somer's Quay.
1852	C. Constable	.	.	.	Lambeth.
1853	J. Finnis	.	.	.	Tower.
1854	D. Hemmings	.	.	.	Bankside.
1855	H. White	.	.	.	Mill Stairs.
1856	G. W. Everson	.	.	.	Greenwich.
1857	T. White	.	.	.	Mill Stairs.
1858	C. J. Turner	.	.	.	Rotherhithe.

1859	C. Farrow, Jun. . . .	Mill Stairs
1860	H. J. M. Phelps . . .	Fulham.
1861	S. Short . . .	Bermondsey.
1862	J. Messenger . .	Cheery Garden Stairs.
1863	T. Young . . .	Rotherhithe.
1864	D. Coombes . .	Horselydown.
1865	J. W. Wood . .	Mill Stairs.
1866	A. Iles . . .	Kew.
1867	H. M. Maxwell . .	Custom House.
1868	A. Egalton . . .	Blackwall.
1869	G. Wright . . .	Bermondsey.
1870	R. Harding . .	Blackwall.
1871	T. J. Mackinney . .	Richmond.
1872	T. G. Green . .	Hammersmith.
1873	H. Messum . .	Richmond.
1874	R. W. Burwood . .	Wapping.
1875	W. Phelps . . .	Putney.
1876	C. T. Bulman . .	Shadwell.
1877	J. Tarryer . .	Rotherhithe.
1878	T. E. Taylor . .	Hermitage Stairs.
1879	H. Cordery . .	Putney.
1880	W. J. Cobb . .	Putney.
1881	G. Claridge . .	Richmond.
1882	H. A. Audsley . .	Waterloo.
1883	J. Lloyd . . .	Chelsea.
1884	C. Phelps . . .	Putney.
1885	J. Mackinney . .	Richmond.
1886	H. Cole . . .	Deptford.
1887	W. G. East . .	Isleworth.
1888	C. R. Harding . .	Chelsea.
1889	G. M. Green . .	Barnes.
1890	J. T. Sansom . .	Strand-on-the Green.
1891	W. A. Barry . .	Victoria Docks.
1892	George Webb . .	Gravesend.
1893	J. Harding, Jun. .	Chelsea.
1894	F. Pearce . . .	Hammersmith.

1895	J. H. Gibson	.	.	.	Putney.
1896	R. J. Carter	.	.	.	Greenwich.
1897	T. Bullman	.	.	.	Shadwell.
1898	A. J. Carter	.	.	.	Greenwich.
1899	J. See	.	.	.	Hammersmith.
1900	J. J. Turffrey	.	.	.	Bankside.
1901	A. H. Brewer	.	.	.	Putney.
1902	R. G. Odell	.	.	.	Lambeth.
1903	E. Barry	.	.	.	Brentford.
1904	W. A. Pizzey	.	.	.	Lambeth.
1905	Henry Silvester	.	.	.	Hammersmith.
1906	E. L. Brewer	.	.	.	Putney.
1907	Alfred Thomas Cook	.	.	.	Hammersmith.

In compiling the above list, as no official record of the winners was kept between 1715 and 1790, I had largely to rely on the perusal of old journals at the British Museum and elsewhere. It is much to be regretted that though I have been able to make several important additions and alterations, this list is not yet as complete as I could wish. The only test of correctness I was able to apply was a negative one, obtained by going to the Watermen's Hall and carefully perusing the list of men who were bound apprentices, in order to see if the name of a given winner were possible or not. The men at that time were bound in apprenticeship for seven years, and were only allowed to row for the trophy during the first year of their freedom; so that a man who came out of his apprenticeship on August 2, 1718, for instance, would be allowed to scull for the Coat and Badge on August 1st, 1719, and the list of men bound in 1711–12 had to be carefully searched to check off the fact that such a man existed, and was out of his time, on the date of the race to which his name has hitherto been appended in the records.

We have been so far unable to trace the name of the first man who won this Coat and Badge; but by the kind permission of the Watermen's Company I was enabled to do something even better in reproducing his portrait, painted shortly after the event, seated in his wherry. For 1716 I was entirely unable to decide between the claims of Edward Bishop and Edward Gullyford. They were both bound apprentices the same year and they both took up their freedom of the river the same year ; half the journals perused give one and half the other. The years 1717 and 1718 also beat me. For 1719 I am enabled for the first time to give the correct name of John Dolbey of Rotherhithe. In 1720, although we know the race was rowed for twice and was eventually won by a man who plied at St. Catherine's Stairs, I have so far been unable to discover his name. In 1721 C. Gurney of Foxhall won the race : this is a new find. The name Gundy has generally been given, an easy mistake to make no doubt. The name was probably hawked from boat to boat at the finish of the contest, and the reporter of that date had no other means of finding out the winner's name, which became corrupted in transmission. This is much more evident in the name of the 1772 winner, which has up to now been handed down as Welloris ; we find Wilmoris, Willmorris and Will Morris, until we get the correct solution of William Morris of Rotherhithe. The years of 1724–5 are missing.

In 1726 there were two races ; the first being a bad start was appealed against and another race rowed, which was won by Thomas Barrow of Sunbury. 1727 is also a blank. In 1728–9 I make no alterations but give a few additions of initials and names of stairs at which they plied. In 1730 J. Burroughs' name used to appear as the winner. This is unmistakably and undoubtedly wrong. John Broughton of Hungerford, the famous prize-fighter, won it that year. In 1737 again there has hitherto appeared to be a doubt as to the correct name of the winner ; J Heaver of Battersea we find to be the man. For 1739 J. Harrington and G. Anderson have both been given as winners, but the correct name was George Harrington of St. Saviour's.

In the same way Winch of Temple Stairs until now has usually been held the winner in 1740, when it should be J. Wing " of Whitefryers." 1742 is again missing. From there to 1753 inclusive I have merely added a few initials and stairs. The 1754 winner is another case of inaccurate reporting. Some of the old

THE FIRST WINNER IN HIS WHERRY.
From the original painting in Watermen's Hall.

journals give Adam and others Maskall, the real man's name being Adam Marshall of St. Saviour's. For 1756 we can get no further than that it was a young man from Cuckolds Point. In 1757 "W. Wright" becomes John White of Putney, and in 1758 J. Langly becomes John Danby of Christ Church. I find the winner's name for 1763 spelt in no less than five different ways. It probably should be S. Eggleton of St. Paul's. For 1764 the name of the winner could not possibly have been Murlin. The name of apprentices eligible to row that year which are at all like Murlin were Martin or perhaps Morton; but as a matter of fact we have perfectly sound evidence from the Fishmongers' Company and other sources that John Morris of Horseferry won that year. The 1765 winner I cannot guarantee, but I fancy, from what we have been able to gather, that it was R. Eggleton of St. Catherine's. In 1770 both Pasby and Goddard appear as winners; Thomas Goddard of Greenwich, however, was undoubtedly the man. In like manner for 1777, as between Pickering and Pender, I award the Coat and Badge to J. Pickering of Greenhithe. The names of James Bowler for 1783 and John Davis for 1784 are new. In 1788 the only correct spelling of the man's name was Thomas Radbourne. I also have my doubts as to the correctness of Byers, in 1790, as a winner. The only names beginning with " B," among any names like this of the men who were free to row that year, were Nicholas Miles Brid and J. Bisco; and harking back to 1782 I cannot find the name of Truck, but must let it stand.

As regards the accounts of the race itself, as will be seen from a fair sample of cuttings given later, the journalistic accounts were mostly very meagre in detail and many were incorrect altogether. In spite of some evidence to the contrary, I think I am correct in stating that the first race took place on August 1, 1715, the first anniversary of King George I's accession to the throne. The *Weekly Journal* for 1766 says that the colour of the Coat was orange, " To the immortal memory of William III who delivered Great Britain from Slavery, Popery, and arbitrary power and bequeathed us the invaluable blessing which we now enjoy, a Protestant King. The silver badge having a horse on it with the motto 'Liberty,' signifies the rights and freedom this nation now possesses under the most auspicious reign of King George whom God grant long to reign." The writer of this must be wrong, as I will show later when describing in detail the Coat and Badge and Doggett's Will.

In the short account of John Broughton I give my reasons fully for saying that he won the Coat and Badge in 1730. In 1720, as I have already remarked, the race was rowed for twice, and the *London Journal* for August 13 of that year says it was won by a young fellow of St. Catherine's, and the man who originally came in second received abundance of foul play or he had carried off the prize, particularly when being very near the goal a boat was run into him which stove in the bows of his wherry. In 1723 again we hear that one of the leaders had his scull knocked away and a big boat was rowed across his bows.

In 1736 Evans, a competitor, was hit with a bottle and nearly killed. In 1752 five of the six were below-bridge men; the sixth John Cook, being above bridge, had his wherry filled with water, and J. Hogdon claimed the Badge, but the Fishmongers' Company ordered it to be rowed again, when Hogdon really won.

So great was the excitement at the finish in 1754 that about a dozen people upset into the river.

Whilst reading the *Life of John Delane*, written by Dasent, I notice that he mentions the fact that at a meeting of the House of Commons in the year 1848, the Speaker left the Chair and the members thronged to the Terrace to watch the race for Doggett's Coat and Badge pass by. I hardly think the present House of Commons would follow this precedent, nowadays, even if they happened to know that it was about to pass, although I observe that the nurses and staff of St. Thomas' Hospital opposite always take great interest in the proceedings. The Terrace of the House of Commons is generally empty.

I should like to remind my readers that the colour of the Coat was undoubtedly orange, and probably has only become red because more red was gradually put into the dye. The Badge has also been altered. But as late as 1853 the Badge was correct, having the wild horse with the word Liberty engraved at the top and the words, " The gift of Mr. Thomas Doggett the late Comedian " underneath. If I may be allowed, I should like to suggest a return to the old original Coat and Badge in accordance with the terms mentioned in Mr. Doggett's will.

There is a picture, now hanging in Mr. Towse's office, in Fishmongers' Hall, of " Happy (or Natty) Jerry," who described himself as a winner of Doggett's prize. If this is true, the date of 1785 has been suggested for him. His portrait is accompanied by some homely but vigorous poetry.

CHAPTER XII

Some Famous Winners

> Now Neptune's offspring, dreadfully serene,
> Of size gigantic and tremendous mien,
> Steps forth, and midst the fated lists appears;
> Reverend his form, but not yet worn with years.
> To him none equal in his youthful day
> With feathered oar to skim the liquid way;
> Or through those straits whose waters stun the ear
> The loaded lighter's bulky weight to steer.
> Soon as the ring their ancient warrior view'd,
> Joy filled their hearts, and thund'ring shouts ensu'd,
> Loud as when o'er Thamesis' gentle flood
> Superior with the Triton youths he rowed;
> While far ahead his winged wherry flew,
> Touched the glad shore, and claimed the Badge, its due.

JOHN, better known as Jack Broughton, of whom the above lines were written by Paul Whitehead in *The Gymnasia* or *Boxing Match* in 1744, was born in 1703.

The book mentioned above was dedicated " To the most puissant and invincible Mr. John Broughton," whose career we give here at some length, because we consider him perhaps the most famous man who ever won the Coat and Badge. Of his early boyhood and training we know nothing. He was bound apprentice rather late in life, at the age of twenty, on May 31, 1723, to Mr. John Martin of Hungerford, and won Doggett's Coat and Badge on August 1, 1730. He was at this time a good-looking, well-set-up man, 5 feet 11 inches in height, and weighed 14 stone. He had, it is said, an open countenance and a sharp penetrating eye, and his form was athletic and commanding, and denoted strength. He took to boxing shortly after his victory in 1730, and quickly rising to fame became champion boxer of England in 1734. He first fought in a booth which was erected at Tottenham Court, in which the proprietor, George Taylor, invited the professors of the art to show their skill and the public to be present at its exhibition. The Tottenham Court booth was the only stage on which these professors or " Masters of the Boxing Art " displayed their powers until Broughton, patronized and encouraged by some of the nobility and gentry, built his amphitheatre in the Oxford Road near the spot where Hanway Street, Oxford Street, now stands, in 1742. This building was opened on March 10, 1743. His battles up till now had been won against such notable champions as Pepes Gretting, George Taylor, George Stevens or the Coachman, Jack James, and others, and so he had fairly earned his title to the championship long before he began running his own amphitheatre in 1743.

Broughton has rightly been styled the father of English boxing. He promulgated a " Code " for the guidance of the combatants and the satisfaction of the judges. His new rules were agreed upon by pugilists and approved of by the gentlemen, on August 18, 1743, and lasted in perfect integrity from then until 1838, a period of nearly a hundred years. He introduced science and humanity into what was up till then a barbarous sport, by not only inventing defensive guards, but also preventing a man being hit when he was down. He also introduced gloves or mufflers for conducting mock combats or sparring matches, his invention being announced in the *Daily Advertiser* of February, 1747, as follows:—

Mr. Broughton proposes with proper assistance to open an academy at his house in the Haymarket, for the instruction of those who are willing to be initiated into the mystery of boxing, where the whole theory and practice of that truly British Art with all the various stops, blows, cross-buttocks, etc., incident to combatants will be fully taught and explained, and that persons of quality and distinction may not be debarred from entering into a course of those lectures they will be given with the utmost tenderness and regard to the delicacy of the frame and constitution of the pupil, for which reason mufflers are provided that will effectually secure them from the inconveniency of black eyes, broken jaws, and bloody noses.

The Duke of Cumberland was his patron and took him travelling on the Continent, and made him a Yeoman of the Guard to the King. We cannot here describe his fights in detail, but on

JOHN BROUGHTON, PRIZE-FIGHTER AND WINNER OF
DOGGETT'S COAT AND BADGE.

Tuesday, April 10, 1750, he attempted untrained to fight Slack, a butcher. After five minutes' fighting odds of 10 to 1 were laid on Broughton, when suddenly Slack got in a lucky blow which closed Broughton's eyes, and Slack beat him in fourteen minutes. He then retired into private life, living at Walcot Place, Lambeth, and became a connoisseur and dealer and buyer of curiosities, old furniture and articles of vertu, as well as of stocks and shares in Change Alley. He died on January 18, 1789, and was buried in Lambeth Church on the 21st inst.

Another famous winner, this time still, fortunately, with us on the river, is William Giles East, who was born at Lambeth on February 2, 1866, migrated to Putney the same year, and was apprenticed to Jimmy Rise of Richmond in 1882. He won the Putney Badge, which was presented by the L.R.C. in the first year of his apprenticeship, i.e. 1882. This badge is open to all watermen's apprentices under the age of twenty-one. He won Doggett's Coat and Badge in 1887, the sculling championship of England in 1891, became a Queen's Waterman on November 4, 1898, and was appointed Bargemaster to the King on June 22, 1906. There used to be forty Royal Watermen; I think, however, there are only thirty left alive now, and as they do not fill the vacancies, it is the intention of the authorities to let the number reduce itself to twelve. Bill East, I need hardly say, is a great favourite with every one who has anything to do with the river. He had the Prince's Head on Richmond Green for thirteen years, and is now ruler over the destinies of the Pigeon Hotel at Richmond. He is also a first-rate oar. He stroked the Champion Four twice to victory in the National Regattas of '90 and '91, won the Champion Pairs with Driver at the same regatta, and later on with the same partner won a £200 match against Corcoran and Kanty from Putney to Mortlake. He is also an excellent coach, and his pupils in the sculling line have frequently won the Diamond and Wingfield Sculls.

We have already noted that John Broughton, the winner of the Coat and Badge, became champion pugilist. Another waterman of Kingston-on-Thames named Lyons became England's

WILLIAM GILES EAST, KING'S BARGEMASTER
AND WINNER OF DOGGETT'S COAT AND BADGE.

champion boxer in 1769. Mr. John Angle, a fine oar and winner of a Grand Challenge Cup Medal under the colours of the Thames R.C., became, as every one knows, the most perfect amateur boxer of his day. Tom King, another boxing champion, became a very fine sculler and won several big matches.

C. R. Harding, who won the Coat and Badge in 1888, became champion sculler of England in 1895; and W. A. Barry, another winner of the Badge in 1891, gained championship honours in 1898.

In looking over the list of winners, and in going over the old lists of apprentices, etc., we note the name and family of Cole, who won in 1821, 1849, and 1886, to be of extreme antiquity. In like manner the name of Phelps, so well known at Putney nowadays, can be traced back to the sixteenth century. They also supply two winners of the Badge, namely, C. Phelps, '84, and H. J. M. Phelps, 1860. It is hardly likely that all the names of England's most renowned scullers would occur among the list of Doggett's winners, because prior to 1873 the six competitors were drawn by lot; and as the candidatures numbered in some cases as many as 300 the odds were decidedly against the chances of the best scullers being included among the lucky six.

T. Cole of Chelsea, who won the Coat and Badge in 1849, became champion of England in 1852, by beating R. Coombes twice in that year for premier honours.

The Eggleton family has produced three winners of the Coat and Badge, and the Morris family a like number. The well-known family of Cobb, of which " Doggett " Cobb is such an excellent example, has provided two winners, in 1880 and 1845; the Carters of Greenwich, two; the Hardings, three; the Brewers and Barrys, two each; and the Whites, three; so that sculling ability anyway seems to run somewhat in families. This I think we may safely assume would be a marked feature of this event, had not the competitors in olden days been chosen by lot. They have not always welcomed reform, as the old song says:

Improvement's march is sure and slow
And never can be stopping;

But that there tunnel was no go,
 Bor'd by Brunel at Wapping.

Confusion and bad luck, I say,
 To all these precious schemers—
May every bridge be swept away,
 And Satan seize the steamers!

CHAPTER XIII

Accounts of the Best Races

[Taken from Contemporary Newspapers.]

1721.

THE same day the Livery and Badge given annually by Mr. Dogget in Honour of the day were rowed for from London Bridge to Chelsea by Six watermen that were out of their time this year, and carry'd by one Gundy of Fox Hall, but we hear that a dispute is likely to arise about their manner of Starting which they say was not regular.

1722.

The same Day Mr. Dogget's Annual Legacy of a Coat and Badge was rowed for, from London-Bridge to Chelsea, by six young Watermen, whose Apprenticeships expired within last Year, and won by a Rotherhith Man.

1723.

The same Day Mr. Dogget's Livery Coat and Badge was rowed for from London-Bridge to Chelsea, by five Watermen newly out of their Time, and won by one Howard who plies at Cupid's-Bridge.

1726.

The same Day Dogget's Livery and Badge were row'd for from London-Bridge to the Swan at Chelsea, by six young Watermen that came out of their Apprenticeships this Year, and won by a below Bridge Man.

We are inform'd that Mr. Dogget's Livery and Badge are to be row'd for over again, there being a Contest about the Watermen's Manner of Starting on the first Instant ; three of whom are said to have put off before the Signal was given.

Yesterday Mr. Dogget's Livery and Badge were row'd for a second Time to decide the Dispute that happen'd about that Affair on the first Instant, and the same were won by a Sunbury Waterman.

1731.

This Day Mr. Dogget's Livery and Badge will be row'd for from London Bridge to Chelsea, by six young Watermen that came out of their Time this last Year.

1736.

Monday about two of the Clock in the afternoon Mr. Dogget's Coat and Badge was rowed for from the Swan at London Bridge by Six young watermen to the Swan at Chelsea, which was won by one Hilliard who plies at Westminster Bridge.

1737.

On Monday next being the Anniversary of the late King's Accession to the Crown, the Coat and Badge which Mr. Dogget left to be annually row'd for in Honour of the Day, will be rowed for from London Bridge to Chelsea, by Six Watermen whose Term of Apprenticeship expired this Year.

1739.

Yesterday Mr. Dogget's Annual Coat and Badge was rowed for from the Old Swan at London-Bridge, to the Swan at Chelsea, by Six young Watermen ; and the same was won by one Harring-ton, Son to Mr. Harrington, at the Swan in Salisbury-Court.

1740.

To-morrow Mr. Dogget's Annual Coat and Badge, which was given in Commemoration of his late Majesty's happy Accession, will be row'd for by 6 Watermen who came out of their Apprentice-ships this Year, from the Old Swan at London-Bridge to the White Swan at Chelsea.

1740.

Yesterday being the Anniversary of his late Majesty King George the First's Accession to the Throne, the Orange Coat and Badge left by the late Mr. Dogget the Comedian to be annually row'd for on that Day by six young Watermen not Twelve Months out of their Apprenticeships, was won by John Winch who plies at the Temple Stairs.

1744.

On Tuesday Mr. Dogget's Coat and Badge was won by Lord Windsor's waterman who plies at Mills Stairs Rotherhith.

1748.

Yesterday Mr. Dogget's Annual Coat and Badge was rowed for by 6 young watermen from the Old Swan at London Bridge to the White Swan at Chelsea, which was won with ease by one Wagdon who plies at Whitefryars Stairs.

1750.

Yesterday Mr. Dogget's annual Coat and Badge was rowed for from the Old Swan at London Bridge to the White Swan at Chelsea and won by John Duncombe who plies at Blackfriars.

1751

We hear that a scheme is on foot to raise a Subscription by the gentlemen who row on the river Thames for a Boat to be given to the man who wins Doggett's Coat and Badge which they intend to continue annually.

1753.

Yesterday Mr. Dogget's Badge and Coat which he left to be rowed for on the 1st of August by Six young watermen from the Old Swan at London Bridge to the White Swan at Chelsea was won by Nathaniel Sandiford of Masons Stairs who was least expected to win it. Tobit Bond of Whitehall Stairs came in second and is entitled to five pounds and Jack Egleston who came in third has three pounds. It was esteemed the best rowing match that has been known for many years.

1754.

On Thursday the annual Coat and Badge given by Mr. Dogget the Comedian was rowed for by Six young watermen just out of their time : two of whom ply at Whitehall : two at the Temple : one at the Old Swan and one below Bridge : it was won by Adam Maskall of the Temple Stairs.

1755.

Yesterday Dogget's Coat and Badge was rowed for by Six young watermen just out of their apprenticeships from the Old Swan to the Swan at Chelsea, and won by Charles Gill who plies at the Old Swan.

1757.

Monday evening the Coat and Badge left by Mr. Dogget the Comedian was won by William Wright of Putney. The two who came in Second and third ply below Bridge.

1760.

Yesterday Mr. Dogget's Coat and Badge was rowed for by Six young watermen who came out of their time this year from the Old Swan near London Bridge to the Swan at Chelsea and was won by Ephraim Wood of New Crane Stairs Wapping.

1761.

Last Saturday evening Mr. Dogget's Coat and Badge was rowed for and won by one Penny a waterman at Richmond.

1763.

Yesterday Doggett's annual Coat and Badge was rowed for by six young watermen from the Old Swan at London Bridge to the White Swan at Chelsea, and was won by Samuel Egglestone who plies at Paul's Wharf.

1764.

Mr. Dogget's Coat and Badge which was rowed for yesterday was won by Mr. Robert Morrice who plies at the Horse-Ferry Westminster, who served his time at Irongate Towerhill: he won by only two or three Boat's length, two more coming in very near.

1766.

Mr. John Sugden ironmonger in Southwark: his skull was fractured two days before by a bottle thrown at him on the Thames, when the Coat and Badge were rowing for.

1772.

Dogget's Coat and Badge rowed for on Saturday the first of August was won by one Briggs who plies at Somerset-Stairs.

1775.

Yesterday according to annual custom Six young watermen
started at the Old Swan to row from thence to the Swan at Chelsea for Dogget's Coat and Badge : five of whom belonged to
stairs below London Bridge and one above viz Lambeth. It was
generally allowed to be as good a match as has been known for
many years. A man belonging to Irongate came in first and was
entitled to the Coat and Badge : The Lambeth man came in
Second who was entitled to £5 and the Third man belonging to
Horsleydown was entitled to £3. They started about one o'clock
at noon, by which means many persons were disappointed as it
was not expected they would set off till about seven in the evening.

1777.

Yesterday the annual prize of a coat and badge left by Mr.
Dogget was rowed for by young watermen from London Bridge
to Chelsea. The Coat and Badge were won by a man at Queenhithe. The £5 by a man at Kings Arms Stairs : and the £3 by
another man at Queenhithe.

Friday evening a gentleman standing in the Steel Yard to see
the watermen row for the coat and badge had his pocket picked
by a genteel young fellow : the mob were for ducking him : but
an impress gally being near at hand, the Gentleman prudently
delivered him into the hands of the Officer to serve his Majesty
who took proper care of him promising he should have a good
birth on board the tender.

1778.

Dogget's Coat and Badge rowed for on Saturday by six young
watermen was won with great ease by Henry Pearson of Hungerford Stairs. Henry Cooper of the Custom-house key was the
second boat and was entitled to £5—Cownden of Wapping Old
Stairs was the third and had £3.

1779.

On Monday the late Mr. Dogget's the Comedian's annual
Coat and Badge which was rowed for by six young watermen was
won by William Boddington who served his time to Mr. Clover

Lighterman and boat merchant Bridewell Precinct ; Wm. Mead who served his time at the Three Cranes came in second and is entitled to £5 and William Hudson of Irongate came in third and is entitled to £3.

1781.

Wednesday being the day appointed for Dogget's Coat and badge being rowed for—a great number of persons assembled on both sides of the water, and the candidates were ready to try their abilities. They started but some foul play being used, they were stopped by the rulers of the Watermen's Company and the next day appointed for the contest. They yesterday accordingly again assembled and without interruption arrived at Chelsea : when —— Reeves of the Hermitage came in first —— Tomlin of Lambeth second and a young fellow of St. Katherines third.

1782.

Thursday Mr. Dogget's annual Coat and Badge was rowed for from the Old Swan London Bridge to the Swan at Chelsea by six young watermen whose time expired this year. They started about 2 o'clock and three of them kept together till they got to Lambeth where one began to get ahead and was soon followed by a second. These two kept pretty nearly abreast of each other till they came pretty nigh the goal when the first man's skull split, which retarded him so much that the second man got in first. The second man is entitled to £5, which is nearly the worth of the Badge. The third gains £3. The name of the winning man is Fricke and plies at Tower Stairs. About 5 o'clock they returned to Watermen's Hall where the prizes were distributed to them.

1787.

Yesterday, according to annual custom, Mr. Dogget, the comedian's legacy, to the Waterman's Company, was rowed for by six young men, whose apprenticeship expired in the present year. The candidates were, John Maynard, of Lambeth ; John Simmons, Bank-side ; William Strahan, Old Swan ; Benjamin Rawlinson, Bank-side; —— Jones, and another whose name we could not learn.

About a quarter before six the signal was given, and the different competitors for the prize started, accompanied by nearly five hundred boats and barges. Between Blackfriars and Westminster bridge, they began to exert their utmost efforts, and Rawlinson arrived first at the Swan at Chelsea, and therefore obtained the Coat and Badge; Maynard second, and is entitled to five pounds; Jones, the third, to three pounds; Simmons fourth, Strahan fifth, and the sixth gave out at Schoolboys Point.

1788.

Friday the Annual Match for Dogget's Coat and Badge was rowed for by six young watermen. The boats that started belonged to the following places:

Wandsworth .	. rowed by	Rathbourne.
Blackfryars .	. ,, ,,	Skewtow.
Old Swan .	. ,, ,,	Babbington.
Pepper Ally Stairs .	. ,, ,,	Boyer.
Hermitage .	. ,, ,,	Carter.
Ratcliffe Cross .	. ,, ,,	Nicholls.

The signal for starting was given from the Old Swan at London Bridge about a quarter before four. Rathbourne soon evinced his superior strength, leaving his competitors a great distance behind and being the first boat that arrived at the Swan Chelsea was the winner of the Coat and Badge. Nicholls arriving second was entitled to £5 and Babbington who was third £3. Boyer gave up the contest off Millbank.

1790.

Yesterday Dogget's Coat and Badge were rowed for by six young watermen: but the unfavourable aspect of the day prevented any numerous appearance of spectators: the prizes were respectively won by Byon, Martin and Atkins.

1793.

Thursday being the 1st of August Dogget's Coat and Badge were rowed for by six young watermen whose apprenticeship has expired this year. They started about 5 o'clock from the Old

Swan London Bridge.   Foster of Lambeth was the first to Hun-
gerford, when Haley of Horsley Down the third till then exerted
himself, passed his competitors and came in first at the Swan at
Chelsea, which entitled him to the Coat and Badge.   Foster of
Lambeth came in second which entitled him to five guineas and
Cordle of Irongate came in third and received three guineas.

1795.

Saturday Dogget's Coat and Badge was rowed for, and not-
withstanding the uncertainty of the weather the sight attracted
a considerable concourse of spectators.   The Coat and Badge
was won by W. M. Perry of Hungerford Stairs.   The second
prize of £5 was gained by —— Finch also of Hungerford Stairs,
and the third by Charles Trickey of Queenhithe by which he
was entitled to £3.

On Saturday evening a thoughtless spectator of the rowing
match on Mill Bank put a lighted pipe of tobacco into a hollow
willow tree by the side of the bank which was not discovered till
it was completely on fire and it was with great difficulty it could
be cut down in time enough to prevent the fire communicating
to the adjoining trees.

1802.

In this year there was a " riot and assault," records of which
are preserved in a Notice, signed by John David Towse, and exhibited in the Company's Hall in 1905 by his grandson, the present
Clerk of the Company.

1806.

On Friday six watermen the term of whose apprenticeship
expired within the course of the past year according to Annual
Custom rowed for Doggett's Coat and Badge, which was won by
—— Brock of Ratcliffe Cross.   The candidates were all below Bridge
men.

1807.
Rowing Match.

Saturday according to annual custom the prize Coat and
Badge bequeathed by Dogget the Comedian was contested by

the six following free watermen : Evans of Tower Stairs, Flowers of Hungerford, Price of Blackfryars, Smith from below Bridge, Sayer of the Three Cranes and Maxfield of Rotherhithe. The competitors started from the Pier-head London Bridge about half past six to row against the tide to the White Swan at Chelsea. When the Boats had however arrived off Westminster-bridge they were fouled by other boats and five of the competitors declined the contest. Evans proceeded to Chelsea but in consequence of the above accident he will not be considered the Victor. The match will be rowed again this day.

1809.

Doggett's Coat and Badge was yesterday rowed for a second time this year in consequence of the first contest on the regular day having been declared foul. It was a most excellent wager. They did not start until about seven o'clock. Barrow and Godfrey took the lead : but they were intent on picking each other up : and at Westminster Bridge young Godfrey of Strand Lane gave in in consequence of having wrenched his shoulder which had been sprained in the original contest when he was the leader. Jury of Hermitage who was the third started forward at Millbank and gained four or five boat lengths in about five minutes. He continued the leader and was first in at the Old Swan at Chelsea at half after eight o'clock.

1812.

DOGGET'S WAGER.

The contest which took place on the 1st of the month for the annual Coat and Badge, left to the free watermen of London, by their old friend Dogget, having remained undecided, in consequence of several accidents which obstructed the race, Friday was appointed for a renewal of the wager. Six young watermen accordingly started from the Swan, below Blackfriar's-bridge, to row to the Swan, at Chelsea. They appeared well matched, and after rowing a short distance, young May, of Westminster, took the lead, and maintained it till they arrived at Chelsea. He, of course, won the coat and badge. Fuller and Reynolds followed in succession, and came in for their respective shares.

1814.

DOGGETT'S COAT AND BADGE.

Thursday the six following young watermen, just out of their apprenticeships, rowed for the Coat and Badge given annually under the will of Mr. Doggett, the comedian. The candidates were—Harris, Bankside; Cooke, Westminster; Butcher, Wandsworth; Humphries, Hermitage; Read, Alderman-stairs; Jones, Vauxhall. The first of August being annually the day on which this rowing-match takes place, it was put off, on the present occasion, on account of the Jubilee in the Parks, until Thursday. At half-past five o'clock, on a signal gun being fired, they started from the Swan, at London-bridge, but, owing to some foul play, they were recalled, and had to start a second time a little before six— the wind and tide were then strong against them. They arrived a quarter before seven at the Old Swan at Chelsea, Harris first, J Cooke second, and Humphries third. The winner was then invested with the coat and badge, the second received five guineas, and the third three guineas.

1815.

DOGGETT'S COAT AND BADGE.

Tuesday being the 1st of August, according to annual custom, the Coat and Badge were rowed for by six young watermen just out of their apprenticeships, according to the will of Mr. Doggett, the Comedian. They were dressed alike, in nankeen jackets and trowsers, and started from the Swan, at London Bridge, about a quarter past four o'clock. The following are the names of the candidates : John Scott, J. Mackay, G. Fisher, W. Anderson, John Sharp, and Thomas Palmer. Scott kept the lead from starting; there was a close struggle between Fisher, Mackay, and Anderson, until they came to Lambeth, where Sharp and Palmer gave in, Anderson and Fisher were then close abreast, and it was doubtful which should win : they continued so during the remainder of the way, and they arrived at a quarter to six, at the Old Swan, Chelsea. Scott first, Mackay, second, and Fisher third, by half a boat. The first boat got the coat and badge, the second five guineas, and the third three guineas.

1817.

DOGGETT'S COAT AND BADGE.

On Friday, the annual Coat and Badge, bequeathed by the will of Mr. Doggett, the comedian, was rowed for by the following six watermen, being the first year after the expiration of their apprenticeship.

John Burton, Westminster.	E. Fletcher, Pickle Herring.
James Robson, Wapping.	J. L. Hambleton, Whitehall.
Henry Fall, Westminster.	G. W. Hix, Westminster.

On the firing of a gun they started from the Old Swan, near the foot of London Bridge, five minutes before six o'clock, against the tide. Hix, of Westminster, took the lead, and kept it until they came off Dowgate, when Robson came alongside of him and a sharp contest took place, till they ran foul of a galliot above Blackfriars Bridge, which detained them until all the boats came up, and a dispute arising, the contest, from the lateness of the hour, was put off to another day.

1818.

The names of the six young Watermen who are to row to-morrow for the Livery and Badge, given by Mr. Thomas Doggett, deceased, a famous Comedian, in commemoration of the happy Accession of the Family of his present Majesty to the Throne of Great Britain:

William Nicholls, Greenwich.	Charles Dean, Horslydown.
George Jones, Paul's Wharf.	Henry And. Mallett, Temple.
Barnaby Windsor, Temple.	Thomas Howell, Westminster.

The second and third Prizes are the Gifts of the late Sir William Joliffe:

	£	s.	d.
The 2nd Prize is	4	7	6
The 3rd Prize is	2	12	6

1820.

DOGGETT'S COAT AND BADGE.

On Tuesday, being the 1st of August, according to the will of Mr. Doggett, six young watermen, just out of their time, rowed for the Coat and Badge. On a given signal, it being nearly low water, they started about a quarter past two o'clock from the Swan, at London Bridge, accompanied by a number of pleasure and other boats. At starting, Grant (of Westminster) was the favourite; he took the lead for some distance, when a severe contest took place between him and Hartley (Strand Land) : they rowed abreast in passing Westminster Bridge, when Franklin (Bankside) became a competitor, and it was doubtful which of the three would be the victor; when off Cumberland Gardens Hartley was about 100 yards ahead, and Franklin and Grant were breast to breast, the other boats were considerably astern. At twenty minutes past three they arrived at the Old Swan, Chelsea, in the following order :—Hartley about 300 yards ahead ; Franklin next ; and Grant 60 yards astern. The other three, perceiving they could not win, hung on their oars, and rowed in at their leisure. The first three received their respective prizes. The second prize is £4 7s. 6d., the third £2 12s. 6d.

1821.

On Wednesday, being the 1st day in August, Dogget's Coat and Badge was rowed for, according to the annual custom, by six young watermen, just out of their apprenticeships. Thomas Cole, of Chelsea, was declared the winner of the livery and badge; William Meckliffe, of Bank Side, came in second, he received £4 7s. 6d. ; Joshua Judge, of Rotherhithe, was third, and received £2 12s. 6d.

1822.

On Thursday, being the 1st of August, the annual prize was contested by six young watermen, who were just out of their time. The combatants started at six o'clock from the Old Swan Stairs, London Bridge, to row up the river, against tide, to the Swan, at Battersea. The prize was won by Noulton, of Lambeth.

1823.

DOGGETT'S COAT AND BADGE.

The Annual Coat and Badge given under the Will of Mr. Doggett, of theatrical celebrity, to be contended for by six young watermen who had just completed their apprenticeship, was rowed for yesterday. The six scullers started from the Old Swan, at London Bridge, at three o'clock in the afternoon, at the firing of a gun. Before they had reached Blackfriars Bridge three were observed to take the lead, which they kept throughout. Their names were Butcher, Braithwaite, and Hallam; the two former belonging to Hungerford Stairs, the latter to Bankside. The race was rendered very interesting from the strenuous exertions mutually made by these young aspirants to pass each other. The two Hungerford men were foremost; and on passing through Vauxhall Bridge, Butcher had convinced most of the amateurs present that he must win it. On his coming abreast of the Old Swan stairs, Chelsea, a little above the Hospital, the report of a carronade on the opposite bank announced to him the agreeable tidings that his labours were concluded. He was loudly cheered by his partisans. The scullers were severally saluted by the firing of a gun on reaching the goal. The discharges, however, of the first three carronades were heard in rapid succession in consequence of the three headmost scullers arriving at the Old Swan nearly at the same time. The weather continued favourable until the race was concluded, which happened about half after four o'clock. There was a good deal of company on the water; but owing to the circumstance of there being but one heat to determine the race, and its being so soon concluded, the number of persons present fell far short of those who witnessed the Sailing Match on Wednesday, or the Rowing Match for the Funny Club prize wherry.

1826.

Another account says :—

" Doggett, the player's, Constitutional Coat and Badge was rowed for according to annual custom, on Tuesday, and won by a man of the name of Boet. The Morning Chronical attributes much of the winner's success to his having been *piloted* by ' Bob Brocking, of Chelsea, who was in a cutter a little astern.' This may be good tactics along the coast of Milbank, but in other parts of the world, the vessel intended to pilot, would in all human probability have gone a little ahead. A prize wherry was also given by the amateurs of Blackfriars, on Wednesday—the Tower wherry on Thursday—and yesterday, a match for a supper, given as an encouragement to industry, by Mr. Lett, the timber merchant of Lambeth."

In 1905 there was posted in Fishmongers' Hall, by the Clerk of the Company, a Notice signed by his grandfather, John David Towse, setting forth a sad story concerning the race of August 1823, and announcing that "We the undernamed, James Cole and William Mount of St. Catherine's Stairs, watermen, and James Reid, of Blackfriars, waterman, with others in a cutter, did wilfully and riotously obstruct two of the wagermen rowing for the said Prize by intentionally running athwart them near Old Swan stairs and stopping their boats with a boathook, whereby they were impeded in contending for the Prize ; and in such act one of the wagermen was struck with the boathook and the whole were obliged to be started a second time." For which outrageous and improper conduct the Fishmongers' Company did very properly punish them.

1827.

A Rowing Match took place on Wednesday for a Coat and Silver Badge, given by Doggett, the comedian, to be rowed for by six pair of sculls, one boat to start from the Swan at London Bridge, and to go to the Swan at Chelsea. It was a very fine match, and was decided as follows :—

Charles Wass .	1
William Phillips	2

The rest were completely distanced.

1832.

DOGGETT'S COAT AND BADGE.

This annual match took place on Wednesday, & as in the three preceding seasons, in the midst of a heavy shower of rain. It was the 114th contest for the livery and badge bequeathed by Mr. T. Doggett, deceased, famous as a comedian, in commemoration of the happy accession of the family of his present Majesty to the throne of Great Britain.   Out of nearly 200 young watermen who were candidates for competition, the following became entitled to row for the prizes, the second and third of the respective amounts of £4 7s. 6d. & £2 12s. 6d. being the gifts of the late Sir W. Joliffe :—Robert Waight, Bankside ; W. Jackson, Richmond ; J. W. Carter, Hermitage ; C. Brockwell, Custom-house ; J. T. Weston, Chelsea ; T. Weed, jun., Bankside.   The distance rowed was from Swan to Swan, against tide.   About half-past six they were started.   Waight took the lead, and maintained it the entire distance ; Jackson was second up to Vauxhall, when Carter went by him, and came in a short distance in the rear of the leading man. Jackson was, however, third, and the others brought up the rear rather stragglingly.

1833.

Thursday, Doggett's Coat and Badge, value £10 were rowed for by five young watermen.   The prize was won by George Maynard, of Nine Elms.   The distance rowed (against tide) was from Old Swan Stairs, London Bridge, to the Old Swan, at Chelsea.

1837.

DOGGETT'S COAT AND BADGE.

The 117th contest for the livery and badge given by Dogget, the comedian, took place on Tuesday last.   Independent of the first prize, the second man received £4 and the third about £2 10s., the interest of South Sea Stock bequeathed by H. Jolliffe.   The day was exceedingly unpropitious, but the contest was a very good one.   The distance was as usual from the Swan at London Bridge to that at Chelsea, and the following had been entered :— William Crew, of Wandsworth, Charles Kitchen, of Horselydown, Thomas Harrison, of Bankside, T. P. Elliss, of the Horse Ferry, George Mode, of Horselydown, and Henry Hopkins of the same place, making three above and three below bridge men.   The distance was, as usual, against tide, and in the start Crew took the lead, but they were altogether.   In making the first shoot young Harrison rowed cleverly, and turned into the shore the

THE RACE IN 1838.

foremost. He rowed admirably, and maintained the distance throughout, winning by about three minutes and a half; Mode was second, and Crew third. Harrison was the winner of the boat at Bankside on Monday last.

1842.

DOGGETT'S COAT AND BADGE.

The annual rowing match for a coat and badge, left by Doggett, the comedian, took place on Thursday. The distance, as usual, was from the Swan, at London Bridge, to the Swan, at Chelsea, five miles against tide. The prize was won by —— Liddy. The other competitors came in thus :—William Wingate, Battersea, 2; John Thomas Sibree, Christchurch, 3; William Tomson, Hungerford, 4; Thomas Savage, Alderman Stairs, 5.

1851.

It has hitherto been the custom for the anniversary of the Watermen and Lightermen's Asylum to be celebrated in the second or third week in June; but in consequence of the many calls on the Lord Mayor's attention, owing to the great influx of strangers in London, and the great Exhibition, he has been unable to fix a time for the festival prior to the 1st of August, when Doggett's Coat and Badge will be rowed for.

1853.

On Monday last, the 1st of August, according to ancient custom, this interesting race—one of the most popular of the season—took place, and was accompanied by a greater number of cutters and other craft than we have seen for some years. The following were the entries :—

John Ormston Kilsby	Bankside.
Richard Babington	Horselydown.
William Barratt	Old Barge House.
James Richard Fennis	Tower.
Rowland Alfred Davies . . .	Battersea.
George Frederick Beckett . . .	Old Barge House.

Mr. Dards, bargemaster of the Fishmongers' Company, was, as heretofore, the manager and umpire, and took his seat in the starting galley, at half-past three, to see the men properly at their

THE RACE IN 1850.

stations at London-bridge, to row against tide to the Swan, at Chelsea. All being in readiness a capital start was effected at ten minutes to 4. Beckett, Davies, and Fennis, being to the southward, had a slight advantage in station, but all were off together, and remained scull and scull for a few strokes. Babington then pulled the nose of his boat slightly in front, closely waited upon by Beckett and Fennis on one side, and Kilsby on the other, in which order they passed through Southwark-bridge, Babington increasing his lead between that and Blackfriars. A beautiful contest was kept up with vigour by Babington, Kilsby, Beckett, and Fennis, the others beginning to tail off, and at Waterloo-bridge the pace began to tell heavily upon Babington, who gave place severally to Kilsby, Fennis, and Beckett. Kilsby now made a most determined effort to get right away from his opponents, but it was met by a similar demonstration of spirit on theirs, and on commencing the shoot off Robert's, it was quite evident that it would soon be ascertained who was the best man. Kilsby held the lead over, but at Vauxhall-bridge it was quite clear that his strength was fast abating, and Fennis, rowing right up to his sculls, in a few strokes afterwards passed him, and never was overtaken, although obviously distressed at the end of the distance, and winning by three lengths only, thus carrying off the livery badge and a guinea. Kilsby was second, three lengths a-head of Beckett, and these two receive £4 10s., and £2 14s. 2d. interest on South Sea Stock, bequeathed by Sir W. Joliffe. Babington was fourth, Barratt fifth, and Davies sixth, which entitled the first named to a guinea and a half, and the last two to a guinea each, which, with the winner's money, are presents by the Fishmongers' Company. The bargemen were regaled with a hearty repast, at the expense of the same company, at the Swan, at Chelsea.

1856.

If we are to be true to the memory of our fathers, it will not do to avoid recording the annual race for Doggett's Coat and Badge. This old established boat race was rowed on Friday week, the course being from the Swan at London Bridge to the Swan at Chelsea. The number of spectators was larger than has been seen

for years before.   There were two men in the race of whom a
great deal was expected, as they had exhibited, even while in their
teens, great proficiency in the art of rowing.   These were Thomas
Coombes, the son of the celebrated Robert Coombes, ex-champion
of the Thames, and William Mansey of Isleworth, but the fortune
of the day was against them.

George William Everson .	Greenwich . . .	1
Charles John Rose . .	Horselydown . . .	2
James Thomas Pockmeal, jun.	Pickle Herring Stairs . .	3
Frederick James Hovey .	Deptford . . .	4
William Mansey . .	Isleworth	5
Thomas Coombes . .	Millbank	6

Everson struck boldly out from the northward with a lead
which he never surrendered, and exhibited a most decided superi-
ority over all the rest, who continued very prettily together to
Southwark Bridge, where Rose commenced fairly establishing
himself in the second place.   Everson won by half a mile.   Coombes
and Mansey both rowed well, but were unfortunately fouled and
much impeded.

1862.

DOGGETT'S COAT AND BADGE.

This ancient and time-honoured wager came off on Friday,
the ever-memorable 1st of August, with its customary paraphernalia
of accompanying cutters, steamboats heavily laden, and thousands
of spectators. Mr. Thomas Doggett originally gave this prize
with the intention of bringing out strong young men, as witness
the race being rowed, four-and-a-half miles, against tide.   Friday
last was just such a day as he would have fixed upon for the race
to be rowed, a true August sun pouring down upon the backs of
the competitors, while a contrary wind out rendered the labour
very hard.   The prizes were as under :—The first man received, in
addition to the coat—or more properly livery—and badge, a
guinea from the Fishmongers' Company, under whose arrangement Mr. Doggett as a member of that company left the match,
and Mr. Frank Towers, of the Victoria Theatre, added to these
the sum of three guineas.   The second and third prizes have for

many years past been the gift of the late Sir William Jolliffe, as per his will, arising from the interest on £260 17s. 3d. Three per Cents Reduced, formerly £200 South Sea Stock, the second prize being five-eighths, i.e. £4 17s. 9d., and the third three-eighths thereof, or £2 18s. 9d., and Mr. Towers added a guinea to each of these; while the usual prizes given to the last men by the Fishmongers' Hall, were to the fourth man £1 11s. 6d., and to the fifth and sixth men one guinea each. To be entitled to row for these prizes it is necessary that all the competitors shall be free watermen, having become such since the wager was last rowed for, and thirty-nine men having sent in their names as desirous of contending, the following were declared to be those who had obtained lots :— viz.,

> James Worrledge, Hungerford.
> Jonathan Oakley, Limehouse Hole.
> John Messenger, Cherry Garden Stairs.
> Thomas James Abbott, Dockhead.
> Edward Olyett, Legal Quays.
> James Richard Beckett, Old Barge House.

For some years past, however, the Fishmongers' Company have allowed any one of the six chosen men, desirous of not competing to dispose of his lot to one of the other applicants, of whom plenty may always be found ready to purchase a chance, and accordingly this year James Worrledge of Hungerford sold his lot to John Bartlett of Horselydown, who contended in his place. The men were at their stations opposite the Old Swan, London Bridge, at the time ordered, half-past five, and they started almost immediately, on the very last dregs of the flood, saving a little tide all the way up. The veteran Mr. Dards, barge-master of the Fishmongers' Company, was the umpire for the twenty-second time, the old gentleman having attended Doggett's Coat and Badge Race for the last fifty-six years. The stations counted from the northward, Bartlett being nearest the Fishmongers' Hall, and the others following in succession, with Beckett on the Surrey side. It was about twenty minutes to six o'clock when Mr. Dards started them, and Bartlett, plying his sculls at rapid pace at once led by a length, but only held his advantage to about opposite

T. Coles in 1853. Champion of the Thames
and Winner of Doggett's Coat and Badge.

Calvert's brewery, where Oakley had gone into the first place, with Abbott close on to him, Bartlett third, Messenger fourth, then Beckett, Olyett last. There were several changes and close sharp struggles among them all to Southwark Bridge ; but here Messenger had begun to lay down to his work, and was passing his opponents one after the other till he came to Oakley, who disputed the point with him, and from here to Blackfriars Bridge the race was very severe, but at Old Barge House, Messenger working from the middle of the river, rowed across Oakley into first place, taking the inside berth on the Surrey shore. About this time Abbott had also gone as near the shore as he could, and was close on to Oakley, and they passed under Waterloo Bridge, Messenger leading by about two lengths, Abbott second, Oakley just astern of him, Bartlett six or seven lengths behind, Beckett and Olyett nowhere. At Hungerford Messenger still led, but not by much, Abbott just heading Oakley, and these positions were maintained till close to Westminster Bridge, when Abbott spurted up on Messenger so fast that it was thought he would go by him ; Messenger went away, however, and Oakley set himself to work to displace Abbott, drawing level with him at the commencement of the House of Lords. The struggle was short but severe, and ended in Oakley going second while they passed a barge, Oakley to the northward and Abbott to the southward, somewhat out of his course. Bartlett was now picking up very fast, and it was a close thing with all. At the Horseferry Bartlett was gaining so rapidly, and rowing so well, that many declared he would win. At this point Abbott was steered very badly right into the Surrey shore, off the end of the Penitentiary, and having to row out to avoid several barges in his course above Vauxhall Bridge Pier, he lost much ground, besides coming in contact with them. This brought Bartlett right on to his quarter and now commenced a very exciting match, Bartlett just drawing in front under Vauxhall Bridge. The race was kept up, Bartlett gradually getting away till he fouled a tier of barges at Pimlico Pier, but immediately afterwards Abbott fouled them more seriously, and was left three lengths astern. Messenger had by this time fully established himself as the winner, and was leading Oakley by six or seven lengths; Oakley double that ahead of Bartlet; Abbott two or three lengths behind him; the others nowhere. Abbott had no sooner cleared himself than he began to lay down to his work in real earnest, and collared his man at Thames Bank Distillery, whence they were fiercely battling to the Victoria Bridge; here Bartlett, putting on a spurt, drew two lengths away, but his boat had been filling with water so fast lately that it was momentarily expected he would be swamped. This naturally favoured Abbott, who, however, had shipped some of the surf, and again he drew level, and a most exciting race occurred between them right home, where Abbott led by about a couple of yards. The following is the order, and as near as we could get it in the din and confusion, the times at which they rowed past the Old Swan at Chelsea, viz:

	M.	S.		M.	S.
Messenger.	37	45	Bartlett	39	40
Oakley.	38	15	Beckett	41	30
Abbott	39	37	Olyett.	41	45

The winner, who is said to weigh but 8 st. 1 lb., was well steered up by Henry Skilton of Bermondsey.

1863.

Almost as we write, on the 12th of February, 1863, the Prince of Wales visits the worshipful company of Fishmongers, in their own magnificent hall at London Bridge. And a newspaper paragraph, describing the festival, says, " With singular appropriateness and good taste, eighteen watermen, who had at various periods since the year 1824, been winners of Doggett's coat and badge, arrayed in the garb which testifies to their prowess, and of which the Fishmongers' Company are trustees, were substituted for the usual military guard of honour in the vestibule."

A more stalwart set of fellows, in more quaintly antique costume, could scarcely be found in any country, to serve as an honorary guard on " the expectancy and rose of the fair state."

1864.

DOGGETT'S COAT AND BADGE.

This exciting annual race, which was established by the late Thomas Doggett (comedian), to celebrate the accession of the House of Hanover to the Throne of England, was rowed on Monday, August 1. The course was from the Old Swan at London Bridge to the Old Swan at Chelsea, a distance of about four miles and a half. The original conditions were that the race should be rowed all the way against tide, but during the last few years the rule has been so much infringed that the competitors have been enabled to save the tide nearly all the way up. The race is for young watermen the first year out of their time, and the following prizes were contended for :—A scarlet livery and silver badge for the winner, to which the Fishmongers' Company add one guinea ; the second man receives £4 17s. 6d., and the third £2 18s. 9d.— the two latter prizes being severally five-eighths and three-eighths of the interest on £260 17s. 3d. Three per Cents Reduced (for-merly £200 South Sea Stock), left by Sir William Joliffe ; the Fishmongers' Company give the fourth man £1 11s. 6d., and the last two a guinea each. The stations count from the Middlesex shore, the man who takes the first lot having the first station, and they follow in the order drawn. The draw, this year was as follows :—Frank Kilsby, T. Wittington, John Henry Darby, W. Wentworth, J. Bury, and J. C. Doo. Of this lot, W. Wentworth and J. Bury disposed of their chances to David Coombes and James Groves, both of Horselydown. Coombes, having bought a chance, came from Dublin expressly to row, and in the mean-time being qualified to row for the Horselydown boat, won the same. Kilsby, from his previous performances in long races, was made the favourite, being from the first instant it was known he had obtained a lot backed at even money against the field. Some spirited betting took place between Coombes and Kilsby, 6 to 4 being laid on the latter, he being much the heavier and stronger man. The betting just previous to starting was 2 to 1 on Kilsby, 5 to 2 against Coombes, and 8 to 1 against any other. Three steamers accompanied the race. The *Lotus, Rifleman,* and *Stork*, each being thoroughly well laden with passengers, and more than the usual crowd of spectators were packed on the wharves on either side of the river and on the bridges, all the way up.   There were a great number of old coat and badge men present, and amongst them we recognised D. Harris, Fogo, H. Campbell, R. Moore, D. Hemmings, Stapleton, etc., etc.   The wind was blowing very freshly from S.W., and down several of the reaches the water was very "lumpy" indeed.   The steamers started from London Bridge about one o'clock, and gradually made their way between the crowd of boats through Blackfriars bridge, where they waited for the racing boats to pass them.   Mr. Dards, the venerable bargemaster of the Fishmongers' Company, who has superintended the race for nearly thirty years, again officiated as starter, and the men, after some little delay, were despatched for the race at twenty-five minutes past one p.m.

The following were the competitors :—

Station.	Name.	Place.		Time.
4.	David Coombes	Horselydown	1	33 min. 12 sec.
1.	Frank Kilsby	Old Barge House	2	34 min. 7 sec.
2.	Thomas Wittington	Legal Quays	3	40 min. 15 sec.
5.	James Groves	Horselydown	4	40 min. 25 sec.
3.	John Henry Darby	Surrey Canal	5	41 min. 20 sec.
6.	George Charles Doo	Mortlake	6	Not timed.

Betting : 2 to 1 on Kilsby, 5 to 2 against Coombes (taken) ; and 8 to 1 against any other (offered).   A capital start was effected, all getting away together, but halfway between the Old Swan and Southwark Bridge, Kilsby came away, followed by Coombes ; the pair making a great gap between themselves and the other four.   Wittington and Groves headed the ruck, Darby fifth, and Doo last of all.   At Southwark Bridge, Kilsby was half a length before Coombes, both, considering the lively condition of the river, rowing at a great pace.   So level and close were the leaders that it appeared almost certain a foul would take place, and Frank Kilsby, when shouted to from his cutter, "eased up," thinking that he could overhaul Coombes at any time.   Master Dave seized the opportunity, and went ahead, followed as soon as possible by his cutter, giving Kilsby as much of their wash as possible.

A desperate race ensued to Blackfriars Bridge between Coombes and Kilsby, the former leading by a length and a half clear, and being so far before the others that all interest in the race was centred in the two first boats. Nearing Blackfriars Bridge, Wittington and Groves fouled, after which Groves took third place, Wittington fourth, Darby fifth, Doo a long way astern. At Waterloo Bridge, Kilsby put on a good spurt and rapidly decreased Coombes's lead, and at Westminster Bridge Coombes, when called upon by his coach, not only put on a good lively stroke, but laughed as he did so. Coombes had now settled down to his work, and his style of rowing strongly reminded us of his father—the ex-Champion—the same quickness being exhibited in the feather, the sharp and effective clip of the water, the steady and powerful lift, and the same full power to the end of the stroke. Kilsby was rowing as well as ever we have seen him, but from the manner he buried his boat and from time to time took in water it is certain he was either underboated or had his work too low. The pace at which the leaders rowed up to the Lambeth Suspension bridge had left the other four almost out of sight. Coombes was leading by six clear lengths at Westminster Bridge, but so persistent was Kilsby in his steady pursuit of his opponent that David had no time to rest. From Lambeth to Vauxhall Bridge, Coombes gradually increased his advantage to ten clear lengths. The wind was now a " dead noser " all through Battersea Reach, and it was thought by the Kilsbyites that their man's extra weight would bring him to the front through the lumpy water, but to their surprise Coombes held his own with apparent ease past Nine Elms and Pimlico Piers. The tide had now dropped, but the ebb had not fairly made, and as the competitors rowed under Chelsea New Bridge they had almost to stop rowing in consequence of the strength of the wind and the roughness of the water. The work was very severe the remaining portion of the distance, but Coombes, if anything, increased his lead, and won by 55 sec. from Frank Kilsby ; the others nowhere. The winner, who accomplished the distance in 33 min. 12 sec., rowed in the celebrated *Antigallican*, built by G. Salter, and was coached up by

George Sinclair, Thames Bank, in an eight-oared cutter, steered by Tom Coombes. Frank Kilsby, who occupied 34 min. 7 sec. in getting the distance, was shown up by his brother, John Kilsby, in the leviathan ten-oared cutter, steered by Horace Cole, of Chelsea. The other competitors came in as above, after a fine race between Wittington and Groves. Wittington was a couple of boat-lengths first passing Lambeth, but rowing very pluckily, was on good terms with Groves halfway to Chelsea New Bridge, and soon afterwards taking the lead, finished third by ten seconds. Darby was fifty-five seconds astern of Groves, and Doo so much behind, that although he finished the distance he was not timed. The prizes were presented in the evening in the usual manner at Fishmongers' Hall.

1865.

DOGGETT'S COAT AND BADGE.

This wager, the oldest established race on record, was rowed on August 1st. Thomas Doggett, the famous comedian, in loyal enthusiasm, founded this race A.D. 1715, to commemorate the accession to the throne of the present house of Hanover. The race was set from the Old Swan, London Bridge, to the New Swan, Chelsea," to be rowed against tide on August 1st for ever." Doggett bequeathed funds to perpetuate his gift, and Sir W. Joliffe added afterwards the interest of £200, three-fifths to the second man, and two-fifths to the third, now funded in the 3 per cents. at £260 17s. 9d. The interest of this sum is allotted to the second man £4 17s. 9d., and to the third £2 18s. 9d. The Fishmongers' Company, under whose management the race is, give £1 1s. to the winner, £1 11s. 6d. to the fourth man, and to the fifth and sixth £1 1s. each, provided they row the distance. The entries are very large annually; but as only six can compete, the names of the competitors are selected by lot. The watermen are, by Doggett's will, to be at the time of the race in the first year of their freedom. The following competed on this occasion :—George Samuel Baker, Mill Stairs, Bermondsey; Charles Lloyd, Horsley-down Stairs; John William Wood, Mill Stairs, Bermondsey; William James Dudley, Lambeth Stairs; Joseph William Brockwell, Lower Custom House Stairs ; Alfred Thomas Ramage, Black-wall Stairs. Mr. Dards, bargemaster of the company, officiated as starter and umpire, and the men started from London Bridge at twenty minutes to three, at the turn of the tide. The number of repairs and constructions at the various bridges on the Thames caused great scrambling amongst the men as they made for the most favourable arches. Brockwell, Dudley, and Ramage ran into each other just below Southwark, and thus allowed Wood to go in front, and to maintain his lead to the end of the race. He led by six lengths at Waterloo Bridge, and maintained this advantage with but little variation to the close. Baker took second place at Southwark, and maintained it. Dudley came up to Brockwell soon after, and came up to Lloyd, but being impeded by boats fell astern again, and came in fourth by five lengths. The race ended as follows :—Wood, 1 ; Baker, 2 ; Lloyd, 3 ; Dudley, 4 ; Brock-well, 5 ; Ramage, 6.

1866.

DOGGETT'S COAT AND BADGE.

England is doubtless the only country in the world which can point to a boat race having taken place year by year over the same course for a century and a half, for similar prizes and under similar conditions, and it says much for the antiquity and vitality of the muscular sports of our nation that the wager established more than a hundred and fifty years since should be still in existence in its original form, and, if not at present attracting the same amount of attention and interest which it commanded in the days when George the First was king, still holding a fair rank among the numer-ous and yearly increasing fixtures of the aquatic world. Our readers are doubtless aware that the race for Doggett's Coat and Badge was established by one Thomas Doggett, a comedian, who, unlike the majority of actors nowadays, was a politician of violent Whig bias, and deeply attached to the Guelph dynasty. In commemora-tion of the succession of the present royal family to the throne of England, he gave the prize of a coat, badge, and freedom to be rowed for annually on August 1 by six watermen's apprentices within a year of the expiration of their apprenticeship. Thomas

Doggett gave no prize beyond that for the first man, but Sir William Jolliffe subsequently added the second and third prizes, arising from the interest on £260 17s. 3d. invested in the Three per Cents. ; the second prize is five-eighths of the interest, £4 17s. 9d. ; the third prize three-eighths, £2 18s. 9d. The first man receives a guinea in addition to the livery, badge, and freedom ; the fourth man, £1 11s. 6d. ; and the two last (provided they go the course), £1 1s. apiece, presented by the Fishmongers' Company.

We have on former occasions called attention to the absurdity of attempting to bring off a race, with any degree of fairness, on the Thames between London and Chelsea Bridges, and, without any undue zeal for the removal of ancient landmarks and time-honoured traditions, cannot but think that the Fishmongers' Company, to whose management the race was left by its founder, would do well to seek " fresh fields and pastures new " higher up the river, where the jolly young waterman might show his skill and dexterity without a perpetual fear of being swamped by the continual passing of river steamboats, whose captains, though laudably anxious to afford the competitors a fair field and no favour, are unable to calm the troubled deeps sufficiently to prevent sundry involuntary shipments of water on the part of the competitors, as was the case with at least two of the men last Thursday, and will be again, as long as the present obsolete course is insisted on. Thomas Doggett gave the prize with the view of producing a good and fair race between the half-dozen apprentices chosen, and it is surely more reasonable to conform to the spirit of his injunctions and transfer the race to Putney, where the race would be moderately free from interruptions, than blindly to adhere to the letter, and continue to start from London Bridge, a *locale* which the increasing extent of river traffic and the number of steamers have combined to render most unfitted for any craft more floaty than a dingey or ship's gig. The following were the competitors for the race, which resulted as follows :—

Station 1.—Arthur Iles, Kew 1
Station 6.—Edward R. Beard, Alderman's Stairs . . 2
Station 2.—James Flower, Poplar 3

Stations count from the Middlesex shore. Mr. Dards, the bargemaster of the Fishmongers' Company, accompanied the race in a cutter, and acted as umpire, a post which he has filled for many years. The custom of rowing against tide has gradually become honoured more in the breach than the observance, and the men were started at a quarter past five p.m., so that they had a drain of tide with them all the way. The course was, as usual, from London Bridge to the Old Swan at Chelsea. The betting on board the steamer was of a somewhat coppery character, dollars and " half-bulls " being the current standard of speculation. Iles, who had the best station, and was also known to be a promising youth, was a hot favourite, having the additional advantages of being shown up by Jockey Driver, and of rowing in a boat of Salters' build, in which Caffin beat Edwards, and which is considered the best specimen of her class. The result justified the confidence of Iles' friends, for, getting well off at the start, he showed a lead of three lengths at Southwark Bridge, and his victory was, in fact, at no time in doubt, as he increased his advantage with apparent ease, and won " anyhow " by " any distance," a vague expression, which in this case may be defined as something about four hundred yards, or nearly a quarter of a mile. Among his less fortunate rivals the race was for some distance interesting, and several changes occurred in the positions of the men, owing, in some measure, to the almost inevitable swamping caused by the swell of the steamer, and to which we have already alluded. At Southwark Bridge, when nearly all the men were seriously inconvenienced by craft, Colpas was second to Iles, but soon, getting his boat full of water, fell astern. Beard ran against a buoy below Paul's Wharf, and was passed by all the others. The men were in very straggling order, passing Waterloo and Hungerford Bridges, Iles having a good lead, and Jones and the others scattered over the river. Atkinson in turn, shipping a lot of water, fell last. Passing Lambeth, the excitement of the spectators on the shore was loudly displayed, although from there being no local candidate it was nothing equal to Coombes and Kilsby's year. At Vauxhall, Beard had drawn up and finally got second. Iles won at the Old Swan, Chelsea, by an enormous distance—about 400 yards—and the others finished in the following order :—Beard, second ; Flower, Jones, Colpas, and Atkinson last. The winner was received with loud cheering, and his victory is a feather in the cap of the up-river division, as Doggett's has hitherto never gone higher than Putney. H. Phelps, of Fulham, won in 1860, and, going back seventy-two years, we find one Franklin, of Putney, recorded the winner, in 1794 ; J. Liddey, of Wandsworth, took the prize in 1842 ; but, with these exceptions, it has never gone further than Chelsea, and the great majority of winners have been below-bridge men.

1866

The eight-oared race between the Leander Club and West-minster School which came off yesterday week, was won by the former by three lengths. The 151st annual race for Doggett's Coat and Badge was won by Iles of Kew, by two or three hundred yards, Beard gaining second honours and Flower third.

1868.

Doggett's Coat and Badge.

The race for Doggett's Coat and Badge and a guinea, and two sums of £4 17s. 9d. and £2 18s. 9d. for second and third man respectively, was decided on Saturday last, from London Bridge to the Old Swan, Chelsea, a distance of five miles. This year there were sixty-five watermen and lightermen between Teddington Lock and Lower Hope in the first year out of their apprenticeship ; and when the draw was made of the half-dozen, the fortnight previous, at Fishmongers' Hall, they were found to be all below-bridge men. The day was favourable, and a smooth and clear course would have been obtained had the race taken place, say, between Putney and Mortlake ; but the going to and fro of steamers at London Bridge renders it impossible for a course to be left open clear of impediments. It is perhaps desirable that the men should have a rough course, so that their watermanship

as well as sculling may be brought into play ; but it is evident that
the fragile craft now rowed in cannot enter into a bumping match
with steamers, or weather the chopped seas kicked up by the latter
about London Bridge. At a quarter to one o'clock the men were
marshalled to their places by Mr. Fred. Dards, jun., bargemaster
of the Fishmongers' Company, who was rowed in an eight steered
by the winner of the Coat and Badge of 1854—D. Hemmings.
They took up their stations (counting from Middlesex side), and
passed the Old Swan, Chelsea, as follows :—

Station.
5.	Alfred Egalton, Blackwall	1
2.	Charles B. Messenger, Cherry Gardens	2
4.	Thos. W. Hawkins, jun., Kidney Stairs, Limehouse .	3
1.	Thos. Day, King Edward Stairs, Wapping . . .	4
6.	Geo. Block, Horselydown	5
3.	Henry Hero Stinger, Rotherhithe	6

The betting on board the two accompanying steamers was 6 to
4 on Egalton, 3 to 1 against Messenger, and 4 to 1 against Hawkins ;
the others did not find backers. After about half an hour's delay
they got off, Egalton and Messenger being the first to row out of
the swell of the steamers, coming scull-and-scull through Southwark Bridge, Day and Hawkins also rowing on together, six lengths
behind. Egalton kept increasing the lead, and Messenger dropped
back, pulling desperately, but awkwardly, two lengths in front of
the other two men, who still held the same relative positions at
Blackfriars Bridge. From here, if the men behind the Blackwall
representative could have sculled well, their chance was certainly
put out by the accompanying steamers giving them all the wash.
Egalton reached the flag-boat in thirty-seven minutes from the
start ; Messenger four minutes after him. Another minute
brought up Hawkins ; and in ten minutes after the winner came
Day. Stinger was not timed, and Block was swamped opposite
Pimlico. George Cannon trained the winner, who shows good
form ; he has fair *physique* for making a sculler, standing 5 ft. 6½ in.,
weighing 9 st. 8 lb., and he obtained his majority four months ago.
Egalton has won two coats and badges at Blackwall, in 1865 and
1866. To say that the race is a test of swiftness with the sculls is

only partially true ; and it certainly does not confer a championship among the apprentices, who have to take their chance in the
lucky-bag before they can enter the lists. The men themselves
do not believe it is a proper test : and the evidence is always forthcoming when the winner receives repeated challenges to row
between Putney and Mortlake.

1872.

DOGGETT'S COAT AND BADGE.

The annual race instituted for young Thames watermen by
Thomas Doggett, the player, in commemoration of the accession
of the House of Hanover to the English throne, came off on Thursday last, Mr. Doggett in his will, directing that it should always be
rowed on the 1st of August. Since the contest was first instituted
various prizes, of which the late Sir W. Jolliffe was one of the
founders, have been provided, in addition to the Coat and Badge,
which is the chief prize of the winner ; and during the last few
years some good men have taken part in the contests, which year
after year attract vast numbers of spectators, not one twentieth of
whom would think of going as far as Putney to witness the meeting
of the best oarsmen of the present day. There is evidently a good
deal in a name ; and some of the proofs of this frequently have
very disagreeable results to the parties concerned, as the number
of steamboats and row-boats which swarm over the course on
such occasions has a tendency to greatly impede, and sometimes
altogether destroy the chances of those competitors who happen to
be a little astern after the first couple of hundred yards. In many
respects the race of Thursday last was a counterpart of most of its
predecessors. There were four heavily laden steamers accompanying it, and the bridges and wharves all along the course—from
the Old Swan at London Bridge, to the Old Swan at Chelsea—
were crowded with spectators, most of whom could have had a
very vague idea as to which was which of the procession of scullers
which the contest generally becomes ere the goal is reached. The
starters—the figures denoting the stations, which counted from
the Middlesex side—were :—(1) Thomas John Lyons, Lambeth ;

(2) Patsy Murphy, Bankside; (3) William Arthur Messenger, Teddington; (4) George Chapman, Horselydown; (5) Thomas George Green, Putney; (6) Joseph Banks, Rotherhithe. Messenger was greatly fancied, and next to him in public estimation was Green, who rowed very strong, and, as will be seen, secured the chief prize, the Teddington man being very unfortunate. A capital start was effected about a quarter-past twelve, Green getting away in the first few strokes, and leading by nearly a length at All Hallows Steamboat Pier, with Chapman, Murphy, and Messenger next. At Cannon-street Bridge, Messenger, whose style was very superior, gained second place, but did not seem at home in the comparatively heavy craft used in these races, and soon afterwards caught the water—which was very lumpy—so badly, that before he could recover himself, all were ahead of him save Lyons, who had not yet shown conspicuously. The young Teddington sculler picked up rapidly after once more getting away, but another crab left him so far astern as practically to be out of the race, which Green, who led by four lengths a little above Blackfriars Bridge, had now in hand. There was a good race between Murphy, Chapman, and Banks, Chapman taking second place at the Temple, and keeping it to the end, Banks and Murphy holding third place alternately to Lambeth, when the Rotherhithe man got clear, the race eventually finishing thus :—Green, 37 min. 40 sec., first ; Chapman, 38 min. 30 sec., second ; Banks, 41 min. 35 sec., third ; Murphy, 42 min. 8 sec., fourth ; Lyons, 42 min. 58 sec., fifth.

Messenger did not row the distance. The winner receives the Coat and Badge and 5 guineas ; second, £4 17s. 9d. ; third, £2 18s. 9d. ; fourth, £1 11s. 6d. ; fifth, £1 1s.

1873.

DOGGETT's COAT AND BADGE.

Yesterday (Friday) evening the annual contest for the coat and badge bequeathed by Thos. Doggett was decided, and, as usual, a numerous company assembled upon the bridges and embankments, whilst the river itself swarmed with a flotilla of small craft of every possible description. The qualification of competitors in this race is that they shall be in the last year of their apprenticeship, and the prizes are as follows :—First prize the coat and badge, with 6 guineas added; second, 5 guineas; third, 3 guineas; fourth, 2 guineas; fifth, £1 11s. 6d.; sixth, £1 6s., provided they row the whole of the distance, and subject to the conditions enforced in previous years. Originally the Coat and Badge was the only prize, but some years later Sir W. Jolliffe left the interest on £260 17s. 3d. Three per Cents. Reduced, formerly £200 South Sea Stock, as second and third prizes, which have since been increased by the Fishmongers' Company and others to the amount mentioned above. The old conditions were that the race should be rowed against the tide, but this rule has been recently done away with, and the competition takes place on the top of the tide. The following are the names of the competitors and the order in which they finished, the stations counting from the Middlesex shore :—

STATION 3.—H. G. Messum (white), Richmond . . .	1
STATION 2.—G. Tarryer (red), Bermondsey . . .	2
STATION 5.—T. W. Christopher (black), Limehouse . .	3
STATION 4.—E. Manning (yellow), Lambeth . . .	4
MIDDLESEX STATION.—B. Buttery (blue), Long Ditton . .	5
SURREY STATION.—G. Beatty (green), Battersea . . .	6

At exactly seven minutes to seven the half-dozen competitors were despatched to an excellent start by Mr. Dards, jun., the barge-master of the Fishmongers' Company, who, as usual, was seated in a galley manned by a crew in the livery of the company. Quickest at getting away Manning showed slightly in front, with Messum second, Buttery third, and Tarryer fourth. At the Cannon-street Railway Bridge Messum had taken the foremost position, and Manning soon afterwards fouling a barge, was passed in turn by Tarryer and Buttery. At Blackfriars Messum was well in front, Buttery second, Tarryer third, Manning fourth, the representative of Battersea being thus early in the race swamped. Going under Waterloo Bridge Messum led by three lengths from Tarryer, who was second, a couple of lengths in advance of the other three,

Manning, Christopher, and Buttery, who were almost level. Steering a very good course, the above bridge representative gradually increased his lead, and off Hungerford Pier was ten lengths to the good, Tarryer still second, and Manning third, the other pair, three lengths in the rear, being hard at it, almost scull to scull, until reaching Westminster Bridge, when Christopher made much the better progress through the lumpy water, and, despite the fact that both he and Buttery were nearly swamped by a tug which had been behaving in a most disgraceful manner all the way, at Vauxhall rapidly drew upon Manning, the Long Ditton representative falling very rapidly in the rear, and ceasing to struggle. The actual result had long ere this been palpably in favour of Messum, who, retaining his lead to the finish, won very easily by 100 yards from Tarryer. Meanwhile a magnificent race was taking place between Christopher and Manning, the latter being about two lengths clear of the Limehouse sculler, and even money was laid that the latter would gain third place. Gradually Christopher drew upon the Lambeth man, and catching him in the last half-dozen lengths, scored third place very cleverly by half a length, being 200 yards in the rear of the second. Taking his own time Buttery completed the distance for fifth money about a quarter of a mile behind Manning. The winner's time was 37 min. 27 sec., as taken by our representative with a centre second top by Benson, and is nearly a minute quicker than last year. It is almost unnecessary to state that the course was from the Old Swan at London Bridge to the Old Swan at Chelsea. Betting previous to the start was evens on Messum against the field.

1874.
Doggett's Coat and Badge.

The annual race, to be the fortunate sculler in which is the ambition of all "jolly young watermen," came off, according to time-honoured custom, on Saturday, Aug. 1, over the old course, from London Bridge to Chelsea. Saturday, especially the Saturday preceding the Bank holiday, is a busy time for railways, river steamers, etc., and London Bridge is hardly so well adapted as a starting place for an aquatic match as the Aqueduct, Putney ; in fact, for some time prior to the start the river was at its busiest, so that it was a difficult matter for the boats accompanying the race to give their occupants a view of the commencement. The preliminary heats had been rowed at Putney a short time previous, a much better plan, by the bye, than the old fashion of drawing lots for the chance of competing, whereby it sometimes happened that the best qualified were left out. It was about 5 o'clock when the competitors were seen making their way to their stations, which were as follows, counting from the Middlesex side :—

1. H. A. Short, Bermondsey.
2. J. T. Phelps, Putney.
3. G. W. P. Curd, Blackwall.
4. W. H. Biffen, Hammersmith.
5. R. W. Burwood, Wapping.
6. J. Freshwater, Deptford.

Mr. Dard, the bargemaster of the Fishmongers' Company, gave the signal by pistol, but many steamers and innumerable small craft were some distance ahead, and kept in front of at least half of the competitors through the whole of the race. Short, Biffen, Curd, and Freshwater got a trifle the best of the start, but at Cannon-street Bridge Burwood had to lay his boat athwart the tide or go under the paddles of a steamer, Freshwater having also to steer out of the way. Shortly after Burwood, Phelps, Biffen, and Curd steering towards one point got in close proximity, and a foul occurred between Curd, Burwood, and Biffen. Burwood and Curd were quickest away, and the former led by about a length at Paul's Wharf, Biffen next, and Curd third. The positions of second and third were reversed by the time they had reached Temple Pier, when Burwood and Curd again came into collision, the former shipping some water, Biffen in close pursuit, and the latter took second place once more just after passing Waterloo Bridge. At Westminster the Wapping youth was still in front, and a good match was being contested between Curd and Biffen, who were about level, Short fourth, and Phelps next. The famous Hammersmith sculler was evidently not so *au fait* to an old-fashioned boat in lumpy water as to a racing craft, and had fallen astern of Curd when they reached Lambeth Palace, about which spot Short's chance was put out by some marsports, who should not have been allowed out in a skiff, and a merciless tug following settled his chance completely. The affair now lay, in point of interest, between Burwood and Curd, as Biffen was a dozen lengths behind at Vauxhall Bridge, and so the race continued, as Curd, although he spurted gamely and repeatedly, could never get within a couple of lengths of the leader, who rowed in determined style, and won by about six lengths from the Blackwall representative. Biffen was third, Short fourth, Phelps fifth, and Freshwater last. The time, as taken by our representative, was 35 min. 15¼ sec.

LIST OF WINNERS OF DOGGETT'S COAT AND BADGE SINCE 1791.

Year.	Name, etc.	
1791	T. Easton	Old Swan.
1792	J. Kettleby	Westminster.
1793	A. Haley	Horselydown.
1794	J. Franklin	Putney.
1795	W. Parry	Hungerford.
1796	J. Thomson	Wapping Old Stairs.
1797	J. Hill	Bankside.
1798	T. Williams	Ratcliff Cross.
1799.	J Dixon	Pageant's Stairs.
1800	J. Burgoyne	Blackfriars.
1801	J. Curtis	Queenhithe.
1802	W. Brown	Limehouse
1803	J. Flower	Hungerford.
1804	C. Gingle	Temple.
1805	T. Johnson	Vauxhall.
1806	J. Goodwin	Ratcliff Cross.
1807	J. Evans	Mill Stairs.
1808	G. Newell	Battle Bridge.
1809	F. Jury	Hermitage.
1810	J. Smart	Strand.
1811	W. Thornton	Hungerford.
1812	R. May	Westminster.
1813	R. Farson	Bankside.
1814	R. Harris	Bankside.
1815	J. Scott	Bankside.
1816	T. Senham	Blackfriars.
1817	J. Robson	Wapping Old Stairs.
1818	W. Nicholls	Greenwich.
1819	W. Emery	Hungerford.
1820	J. Hartley	Strand.
1821	T. Cole, sen.	Chelsea.
1822	W. Noulton	Lambeth.
1823	G. Butcher	Hungerford.
1824	G. Fogo	Battle Bridge.
1825	G. Staples	Battle Bridge.

Year.	Name, etc.	
1826	J. Poett	Bankside.
1827	J. Voss	Fountain Stairs.
1828	R. Mallett	Lambeth.
1829	S. Stubbs	Old Barge House.
1830	W. Butler	Vauxhall.
1831	R. Oliver	Deptford.
1832.	R. Waight	Bankside.
1833	G. Maynard	Lambeth.
1834	W. Tomlinson	Whitehall.
1835	W. Dyson	Kidney Stairs.
1836	J. Morris	Horselydown.
1837	T. Harrison	Bankside.
1838	S. Bridge	Kidney Stairs.
1839	T. Goodrum	Vauxhall Stairs.
1840	W. Hawkins	Kidney Stairs.
1841	R. Moore	Surrey Canal.
1842	J. Liddey	Wandsworth.
1843	J. Fry	Kidney Stairs.
1844	F. Lett	Lambeth.
1845	J. Cobb	Greenwich.
1846	J. Wing	Pimlico.
1847	W. Ellis	Westminster.
1848	J. Ash	Rotherhithe.
1849	T. Cole, jun.	Chelsea.
1850	W. H. Campbell	Westminster.
1851	G. Wiggett	Somers Quay.
1852	C. Constable	Lambeth.
1853	J. Finnis	Tower.
1854	D. Hemmings	Bankside.
1855	H. White	Mill Stairs.
1856	G. W. Everson	Greenwich.
1857	T. White	Mill Stairs.
1858	C. J. Turner	Rotherhithe.
1859	C. Farrow, jun.	Mill Stairs.
1860	H. J. M. Phelps	Fulham.
1861	S. Short	Fountain Stairs.
1862	J. Messenger	Cherry Garden Stairs.
1863	T. Young	Rotherhithe.
1864	D. Coombes	Horselydown.
1865	J. W. Wood	Mill Stairs.
1866	A. Isles	Kew.
1867	H. W. Maxwell	Custom House.
1868	A. Egalton	Blackwall.
1869	G. Wright	Bermondsey.
1870	R. Harding	Blackwall.
1871	T. J. Mackinney	Richmond.
1872	T. G. Green	Putney.
1873	H. G. Messum	Richmond.
1874	R. W. Burwood	Wapping.

THE FINISH OF THE RACE IN 1878.

[We have received a letter from W. Biffen of Hammersmith, who complains that the regulations of this wager, as contained in the printed form supplied to the competitors, were not enforced. One of the rules is to the effect that, in case of any unfair play by any of the wager men or others, the wager shall immediately cease, if the umpire think fit, and the prize shall be rowed for again. Biffen declares that he was fouled no less than five times during the race, once by Phelps, who was afterwards stopped by a steam-boat ; then by Short, and three times by Curd, the last named of whom knocked a hole in both ends of his boat. In addition to this, Biffen states that he was stopped by a barge, and again by a skiff, and that the umpire himself kept his eight right in front of him for upwards of a mile.]

1877.

Doggett's Coat and Badge were won on Wednesday evening by John Tarryer, of Rotherhithe, ten lengths separating him from the second, Charles Collins, of Wapping Dock.

1889.

It is a hundred and seventy-four years since Thomas Doggett, the old Whig comedian, founded the race for six young watermen, which is rowed from London Bridge to Chelsea on the Yule of August. In the Drury Lane Playbill on 1st August 1715, ap-peared an advertisement in these words :—" This being the day of His Majesty's happy accession to the throne, there will be given by Mr. Doggett an orange-coloured livery, with a badge representing liberty, to be rowed for by six young watermen that are out of their time within the year past. They are to row from London Bridge to Chelsea. It will be continued annually on the same day for ever. They are to start exactly at four o'clock." Although its surroundings have been altered out of recognition, the race still represents one of the most curious survivals that have come down to us from the last century. The Fishmongers' Company, which has administered the trust vested in it by his will, since Doggett's death has purposely preserved its character. It is, for instance, still rowed in old-fashioned wager boats, which are, according to ancient custom, solemnly "viewed" by the Wardens in the middle of July. A special "Court" of the Company is summoned for the purpose of starting the Competitors; and the bargemaster—a very old English functionary—is the Umpire. The course, too, is still from London Bridge to Chelsea. The famous "Old Swan"—where people used to land and walk to the other side of London Bridge rather than run the risk of "shooting the bridge"—is still the starting-point as it was in 1715. But the old winning-post, the Swan Inn, Chelsea (where Charles Dibdin's "Jolly Young Waterman" won not only the Coat but a wife), has long been demolished, and its very site was swept away when the Thames Embankment was built in 1873. The flag boat is now moored off the Cadogan Pier. The "orange-coloured livery" with its silver badge—on which is engraved the Hanoverian horse—although, of course, the chief, is by no means the only prize in this contest. There are, indeed, veritably "no blanks," since, as in most regattas nowadays, all the candidates in this race get prizes. Various sums of money have been left from time to time for the purpose, and now the winner gets, as well as the coat, ten pounds, while the five other competitors receive sums varying from one to two pounds. It is, therefore, in these days, when Thames watermen are doubly in danger of finding that "their occupation's gone," no wonder that the contest should still be popular, or that the number of entries should now be so large that the trial heats have to be rowed off at some earlier date, and only the six winners row in the race.

1893.

The annual race for Doggett's Coat and Badge which took place on Friday in last week, was rather spoilt by the mishap sketched by a P.I.P. Artist. The course, which is from London Bridge to Chelsea, is always full of dangers, and this time T. H. Robinson, of Putney, when leading by four lengths struck something floating on the surface, and capsized. This enabled J. Harding, jun., of Chelsea, to finish first, amid the plaudits of his neighbours assembled. That the race is a severe test may be judged from the fact that the time of the winner was 36 min. 14 sec.

The national regatta takes place on Friday next, the 11th inst.

1901.

DOGGETT'S COAT AND BADGE.

The annual race for Doggett's Coat and Badge was rowed on Thursday from Old Swan Pier, London Bridge, to the Swan at Chelsea. The contestants are duly qualified young watermen, just out of their apprenticeship, the Worshipful Company of Fishmongers arranging the race for them. The race was rowed in beautiful weather, six scullers starting for the prize, each wearing a distinguishing colour, in stations, counting from the Middlesex shore as follows :—Alfred Horace Brewer, of Putney (White) ; William White, of Lambeth (Yellow) ; James Bowering, of Wandsworth (Red) ; E. S. Hunter, of Bankside (Pink) ; Henry T. Webb, of Gravesend (Blue) ; and H. G. Hayden, of Lambeth (Green). The starting pistol was fired by the Fishmongers' Company's bargemaster at two p.m., and all the men got well away. Brewer was fully expected to win, and he did not disappoint his friends, for he came in 12 lengths ahead, his time being 29 min. 39 sec. Webb was second and Hayden third. Bowering's craft capsized just after shooting Hungerford Bridge, and he had a narrow escape from drowning. After being rescued he persisted in sculling over the course.

1902.

The oldest trophy that has been competed for year after year without intermission is to be found in the domain of aquatic sport. This is Doggett's Coat and Badge, which was instituted by one Thomas Doggett an actor in the year 1716, and has been competed for every 1st of August—unless that day happened to be Sunday, when the race was held on the following day—down to the present time. The " coat " is, in fact, a complete uniform of the style in vogue among watermen in Doggett's day, and the " badge " is of silver, and is worn on the arm ; it bears an impression of a wild horse—the coat of arms of the house of Hanover —and an inscription.

1903.

Doggett's " Wager."

Coat and Badge won by a promising Sculler.

The race for Doggett's Coat and Badge, which was established as far back as 1716, was decided on Saturday over the usual course on the Thames between London Bridge and Chelsea Pier, and resulted in the victory of Ernest Barry, of Brentford, who scored in decisive fashion from five other competitors.

A start was made on the young flood tide, so that although they had not too much water, the competitors were not troubled with a lot of traffic. Still there were a lot of moored craft in places, so that the young watermen had plenty of opportunities to shew their watermanship, which it may be observed was generally of the finished order.

Fears were expressed before the race that there might be some mishaps at Vauxhall through the bridge building operations, but these proved groundless, as beyond that T. E. Bassett went overboard in rounding to his starting skiff before the race there was not a single accident throughout the afternoon.

A well-known amateur, on the first occasion that he witnessed a Doggett's contest, remarked that it was the " most sporting race he ever saw in his life."

This encomium was perfectly justified on Saturday, especially in the case of the winner, who, sculling in superb style, went to he front at the start, and after taking the Surrey shore and threading his way through a regular labyrinth of moored barges and other craft, emerged safely below Waterloo Bridge, shot over to the Middlesex side, and, never being approached, won easily from F. T. Turk, of Kingston, in 29 min. 44 sec.

Barry is a finely built young man standing about 6 ft. in height, a brother of W. A. Barry (ex-champion), who won this race in 1891. He had already rowed in various rumtum handicaps, and should with ordinary improvement become one of the fastest scullers seen in England for a long time.

The *Queen Elizabeth* carried the members of the Fishmongers'

Company and their friends, and there was also a large following of other craft.

1903.
THE OLDEST DOGGETT WINNER.

" Old Knacker," otherwise Fred Lett, who won Doggett's Coat and Badge so long ago as 1844, and who died on 28th October at the age of 84, is to be buried with musical honours to-morrow.

Watermen, lightermen, and Thames watchmen, will gather at Gainsford Street, Horselydown (just off the Tower Bridge), at half-past one, and accompany the coffin with their bands and banners, all the way to Nunhead Cemetery.

" Old Knacker " worked as a lighterman at Horselydown until within nine weeks of his death. He was always in the fore in philanthropic work among his comrades, and used to attend benefit concerts and the like in his scarlet coat with the heavy silver badge on the arm of it.

All who appreciated his charitable work are invited to attend when the last honours are paid him.

1904.
DOGGETT'S COAT AND BADGE.

The annual race for Doggett's Coat and Badge wager, controlled by the Fishmongers' Company, was rowed on Wednesday on the Thames, between London Bridge and Chelsea, a distance of five miles. It is a contest for young watermen just out of their apprenticeship, and always evokes a lively interest amongst the " bargee " fraternity.

Everything was favourable for this year's struggle, as although there was a head wind in certain reaches of the river, the tide flowed longer than usual, and helped the scullers practically all the way, a condition of things not usually anticipated.

The start was as follows, starts counting from the Middlesex shore :—W. C. Gobbett (Poplar), F. W. Burwood (West Ham), H. J. Macfarlane (Stepney), E. F. Cox (Rotherhithe), W. A. Pizzey (Lambeth), A. B. Burgin (Barking).

Burwood got best away and shewed with the lead for a minute

or so, when Pizzey, on the Surrey side, was joined by Gobbett from the other extreme. These two joining issue, soon drew away from the rest of the field except Burwood, and fought out the result in stern fashion to the end. Gobbett got in front once, but as the pair shot Waterloo Bridge the Lambeth man was once more with the lead, and although Gobbett had his chance of winning the race after this point, and finished strong and well, he steered a very eratic course and was eventually beaten by two lengths.

The positions of the competitors at the finish were :—Pizzey, 30 min. 52 sec., first ; Gobbett, 31 min. 2 sec., second ; Burwood, 32 min. 15 sec., third ; Burgin, 32 min. 3 sec., fourth ; Cox, 34 min. 51 sec., fifth ; Macfarlane, 36 min. 50 sec., sixth.

1905.

Henry Silvester, of Hammersmith, won Doggett's Coat and Badge this year after one of the most interesting races ever seen for this historic trophy. He wore red colours, and drew the fifth station at the start. Among the spectators were members of the European Statistical Society, representing ten different nations, who were entertained to lunch in the Fish-mongers' Hall, and followed the race on board the steamer *Queen Elizabeth*, which started from the Old Swan Pier soon after two o'clock. Some delay was caused by a false start, but at length Pocock, the Company's bargemaster, got them all away on a tide which was flowing up rather slowly. Silvester took the lead on the Surrey side, which proved a great advantage. He was fol-lowed across by all the others except Moss of Bermondsey, who lost way by having to go round some barges. At Blackfriars, however, he was close to the leader, with Peasley of Richmond a good third, the rest distanced so far that the steamer had to wait, and interest centred in the fight for fourth place. Johnson of Lambeth over-hauled Jones of Bankside, but could not catch Reuben Webb of Woolwich, who raced hard to keep him off past the terrace of the House of Commons, where a number of Members were looking on. Johnson was soon afterwards nearly upset by the wash of a steam-tug, but struggled on and finished fourth, after beating Webb

TWENTY WINNERS OF DOGGETT'S COAT AND BADGE.

1868 A. EAGLETON. 1869 G. WRIGHT. 1874 R. W. BURWOOD. 1875 W. PHELPS. 1877 J. TARRYER. 1878 T. E. TAYLOR. 1870 H. CORDERY. 1880 W. J. COBB.

1884 C. PHELPS. 1886 H. COLE. 1888 C. R. HARDING. 1889 G. M. GREEN.

1890 J. T. G. SANSON. 1892 G. WEBB. 1896 R. J. CARTER. 1897 T. BULLMAN. 1898 A. J. CARTER. 1900 J. J. TURFFERY. 1902 R. G. ODELL. 1904 W. A. PIZZEY.

very gravely on the post. Silvester won fairly easily in 32 min. 8 seconds.

1906.

On August 3rd the race for Doggett's Coat and Badge was rowed in very bad water indeed. Luckily only one competitor upset, and he was so quickly got into his boat again that he went on and finished fourth. Brewer of Putney drew the best station on the Surrey side, but did not get a decisive lead until Waterloo Bridge, after which he made straight for the Middlesex shore and secured a long advantage. At this point, Cobb, who rowed in a wager-boat kept in trust by R. H. Forster (Captain of the Thames Rowing Club) for Putney competitors, was a good second, wearing blue, with Dyckhoff of Erith close behind him, and the others not far off. The leader was never caught again, and Dyckhoff had a fine fight with Cobb for second place, but was knocked out of his boat by a big roller at the height of the struggle. He pluckily went on as soon as he was seated again, but came in fourth, being passed by Bushnell of Richmond while he was in the water. Down Chelsea Embankment the river, which had been rough all the way, grew so stormy that it was doubtful whether Brewer could get through ; but he won a well-deserved victory after a good race, which was fairly sculled from end to end of a tiring course. The two other competitors were Carder of Christchurch and Fell of Chiswick.

1907.

On July 24th the race for Doggett's Coat and Badge was sculled from London Bridge to Chelsea, and won after a punishing contest by Alfred Thomas Cook of Hammersmith, who was only about four lengths ahead at the end of the 4¾ miles, or more. At the word " Go," Williams of Greenwich went ahead and Jones of Limehouse was last, a position he contentedly maintained throughout. Under Southwark Bridge, Cobb of Putney and Reid of Bankside got too close and all the others stayed in a bunch in midstream, with Jones by himself on the Surrey side behind some barges until the traffic drove him back again. At Blackfriars Bridge the five leaders were still close together, until Cobb left them in the waves and sought shelter under the Surrey shore until he reached Charing Cross Bridge, well ahead of Reid, in 7 min. 24 sec. At Westminster Bridge Cobb was still ahead, but during the slant across to Middlesex he was passed by Johnson of Putney and by Cook. The latter led at Vauxhall Bridge, in 17 min. 48 sec., and finally won in 27 min. 55 sec. from Johnson, with Williams of Greenwich, Reid, Cobb and Jones behind him in that order. The men used racing outriggers for the first time instead of the wager-boats of previous years.

THE START OF THE RACE IN 1906.

CHAPTER XIV

Other Thames Wagers

> Vith these new bridges and vith steam
> Folks kick up such a fuss,
> There's scarce a WHERRY in the stream,
> 'Tis WERRY hard on us.

IT may be interesting to note a few of the more famous wagers, besides Doggett's race, which used to be competed for on the Thames. The following is a good example in 1723.

Yesterday being the Anniversary of the Birth-Day of the late King William of Immortal Memory, Colonel Williamson, Lieutenant-Governor of the Tower, gave a Boat and Oars to be Rowed for, by 8 Batchelors, Watermen of the Tower Liberties, who started at 10 a-Clock from Wapping New-Stairs, rowed thro' Bridge to White-hall, and back again to the Tower Water-Gate; each Pair of Oars being distinguish'd by their Caps, of Red, Blue, Black and Yellow; and the first mention'd Colour won it, viz. Samuel Lecounts and Richard Wright, who afterwards went to the Tower and demanded the Prize, and had it deliver'd to them at the Parade; and were, with the two that came in Seconds, triumphantly carry'd out in the said Boat upon Men's Shoulders, Rowing in the Air.

Other races were evidently given a fillip by Doggett's yearly match. There was one brought off on May 25, 1748, on the twelfth anniversary of the birth of Prince George, afterwards George III. His father, H.R.H. the Prince of Wales, gave a silver cup to the value of twenty-five guineas to be rowed for by seven boats with a pair of oars each from Whitehall to Putney. They started about 7 p.m., and kept so close together all the way that there was scarce more than a boat's length distance between any two of them. A great number of the nobility and gentry appeared in barges elegantly decorated with pennants and streamers, etc., and rowed by watermen in handsome uniforms. Their Royal Highnesses the Prince and Princess, preceded by a barge in which was a complete band of music, were rowed in a barge ahead of the wager men, followed by Prince George and the young Princesses, all in a newly built barge after the Venetian manner with the watermen dressed in Chinese habits, which made a splendid appearance. The number of galleys attending rowed by young gentlemen in neat uniform gave an air of joy and festivity to the whole. The river was crowded with company in watermen's boats all to witness the same.

Then in 1775, June 23, we have the famous regatta, which was attended by about two hundred thousand spectators, including the Duke of Gloucester. Lord Cholmondeley and the Duchess of Bolton went on board His Royal Highness' barge at Somerset Stairs. The Duke of Cumberland was also present, with the Hon. Miss Luttrell, Lord North, the Prime Minister, the French, Spanish, Prussian, Russian and Neapolitan Ambassadors, and others. The racing was confined (as in the contest for Doggett's Coat and Badge) to members of the Watermen's Company in the first year of their freedom. There were two hundred entries, and twenty-four of them were selected by lot to row. They were given ten days to train in. Twelve pairs were made up, and the course was from Westminster Bridge round a moored boat off Watermen's Hall and back again to the bridge. Four boats started in each heat, and the prizes were for the first pair a new boat with furniture complete, coat and badges, and an ensign with the word " Regatta " in gold letters inscribed thereon, the second eight guineas each, the third five guineas each, and for every other competitor who rowed the full course half a guinea with permission to be in Ranelagh Gardens in their uniform during their entertainments.

On August 16, 1786, there was yet another regatta held on the Thames, when a new wherry was offered as the first prize, two guineas were given to the second boat and one guinea to the third. No less than one hundred watermen sent in their names as candidates, and seven pairs were again chosen by a ballot. The course was from Blackfriars to Chelsea, and back to Vauxhall Stairs. The wherry was won by William Dawsley of Vauxhall, while William Saratt, W. Morton and John Huntley were second, John Hogan and William Oakley third.

The competitors rowed in such uncomfortable garments as white waistcoats, blue silk sashes with white caps. The race was followed by numbers of eight, six and four-oared cutters and many other boats.

Again in Strutt's *Sports and Pastimes* we learn that in 1799 the proprietors of Vauxhall Gardens and Astley's, as the chief method of access was by river, showed some regard for aquatic amusement, and gave annually a new wherry to be rowed for by the jolly young watermen or Thames apprentices, two being in each boat, which was extended to two or three heats or trials before the successful candidate was determined.

On August 8, 1768, prizes to the value of five guineas to the first, two guineas to the second, and to four others half a guinea each, were given by the King for six young watermen to compete for and the first to come in was Roger Petch.

In 1755 a new coat and badge, given by the Society of the Anti-Gallicans in honour of the Prince's birthday, was rowed for by six young watermen from Westminster Bridge to Battersea, and was won by Charles Bernard of Whitehall.

In 1722 a grand regatta on the Thames was promoted by the West End Clubs for June 23. No person was to be admitted to Ranelagh Gardens unless he belonged to one of the following Clubs : Boodles, Whites, Stapletons, Almacks, Savoir-Vivre or Goosetree's.

Twelve boats, each rowed by two young watermen, who had come out of their apprenticeship since June, 1772, were to set off from Westminster Bridge to row round a vessel moored off Watermen's Hall and back to Westminster.

The first men had ten guineas with coats and badges, the second seven guineas each with coats and badges of an inferior value, the third men five guineas each with coats and badges of less value than the second. Every successful waterman to have an ensign given him to wear one year on the Thames. No less than three hundred watermen attended at Mr. Robert's, Lambeth, in order that lots might be cast to ascertain the twenty-four to row for the prizes.

We mention these because in nearly every case they followed Doggett's example in limiting the number of contestants to six. They drew lots for the right of competing. Money prizes as well as coats and badges were given. They were usually for young watermen during the first year of their freedom from apprenticeship. Among later coats and badges should be mentioned the one given by Evan Morris of the Temple. In 1843 he instituted a match for a coat and silver badge with the freedom of the Company, to be rowed for in competition by watermen apprentices in the sixth or seventh year of their time, and this he continued annually until 1850, when it was continued annually by the Leander Club, but has now fallen into disuse.

The only record I have found of any actor besides Mr. Thomas Doggett interesting himself in matters aquatic was in 1825, when the famous Mr. Kean gave a prize wherry, which was rowed for by seven pairs of oars, the course being from Westminster Bridge round a boat moored at Lawn Cottage and back down to the Red House at Battersea.

The Royal Coburg Theatre, when under the patronage of His Royal Highness Prince Leopold of Saxe-Coburg, gave a prize wherry to be rowed for by the watermen of Blackfriars and Waterloo Bridges.

The London R. C. coat and badge exists no more, but there is one rowed for annually at Greenwich, Richmond, Twickenham, Kingston and Putney.

By the KING'S BARGEHOUSE near LAMBETH CHURCH.

APPENDIX I

EPITOME OF THE COMEDY OF "THE COUNTRY WAKE"

By Thomas Doggett

The play begins with the meeting of Ned Woodvill and Frank Friendly, who tells him of his father's death, without a penny of inheritance behind him. Ned thinks of enlisting as his only chance of a livelihood. The scene changes to Sir Thomas Testie's house, where the choleric old Knight is berating his niece Lucia about the acquaintance grown up between his daughter and Frank Friendly.

"Dares he," shouts the enraged father, "without my Leave make love to her under my roof ? Were he a Prince and would endow her like a Queen, and should but think of such a thing without my License, I would lock her up till the Green-sickness had made her eat her passage to him thro' the wall."

Flora comes in when he goes out, and determines to give free play to her love as soon as she knows that Friendly has not spoken to her father, " for the pleasure of what thou call'st Disobedience." So she sends for her lover to meet her at the garden door that night. At that very hour, Lady Testie (far from contented with her " withered carcass " of a husband) comes out to talk with her maid about the handsome stranger who had just ridden down from London. The man himself, none other than Ned Woodvill, as the sagacious reader guesses, comes to the garden gate by mistake for the main entrance while they are talking, and they have just time to put on their masks. The gallant makes immediate proposals, without loss of time, to both of them, and is forthwith walked away by the pair, without the least reluctance.

Friendly manages to have an equally satisfactory interview with Flora, when Sir Thomas discovers her absence and comes hurrying down the garden just after they have plighted troth and gone. But Betty, the very moral of a wicked, sympathetic little soubrette, dispels his suspicions about both wife and daughter, and finally introduces Woodvill as her own swain. Sir Thomas, somewhat extravagantly punctilious, insists on their immediate marriage, but consents to postpone the ceremony till the morning, and leaves the somewhat bewildered man with his niece and daughter, whom he promptly imagines to be the two masked ladies he had first met. But both girls laugh heartily at the proposals he thus mistakenly—but very clearly—makes to them;

and only the return of the maid, Betty, disentangles the situation. She leads him to his room with a hint no audience could misunderstand that he is not to be alone in it all night.

Thomas Doggett, himself, in the part of young Hob, only appears in the third act, as a stupid countryman, to whom Friendly entrusts a letter for Flora, to be delivered without fail that night. This he promises to do, after much argument as to the supposed ghost of a suicide in the orchard, and the dangers of the errand.

This is the scene chosen by Leguerre for his first engraving, but the personages introduced are of course not portraits of the original actors, and Cibber added a verse or two for Hob in his later version.

It is followed by a dialogue which might perhaps lend itself, in more censorious days, to those undesirable criticisms which are so vehemently repelled in Doggett's Dedication and Prologue. For the audience now behold (as well as they may) a dark room in the house, with the impatient Woodvill in a nightgown, " to whom enters " Lady Testie, also " in a nightgown." After a short dialogue, the curtain very properly descends, and I fear that Thomas Doggett would have had little chance of producing a comedy of this kind publicly with so much success in the London of this present year of grace.

Sir Thomas, meanwhile, prowling about the premises on the watch for his daughter's admirer, comes on Hob, with the letter, and beats him soundly for his pains.

I suppose even the long night just described must have at some time ended, though there are no stage directions ; so it must be early the next morning when Lucia appears, in anxious conversation with her cousin Flora about the charming stranger (Woodvill) who has captured her heart at first sight, though he appeared so unaccountably to be enamoured of the maid. They are interrupted by Hob (friend Doggett) with some country people carrying " a Man Dead-drunk," and the scene with Hob and his neighbours follows which I have already transcribed in the text of this book.

The fourth act opens with a dialogue between Friendly and Woodvill, who still has no notion which of the ladies proved so susceptible to his charms, and this is followed by the Fair, or Country Wake, in front of Sir Thomas Testie's house, which gives its name to the piece. Friendly disguises himself as a ballad singer, and Flora looks on, with Lucia, from a balcony. It must have been an animated scene, and Leguerre chooses Hob's recognition of the gentlemen in the crowd as the subject for his fifth engraving. Hob brings out ale, bread and cheese, pipes, and tobacco from his father's inn, and then merrily supervises the country dances that begin at Sir Thomas' request. These are followed by cudgel-play for a new hat with a favour. Hob, of course, is Gloucestershire's champion against any Somersetshire man that cares to try a bout, and promptly breaks Roger's head, to begin with. Sir Thomas is enraged at the result, and leaves the balcony to come down into the fray.

" Let 'en come and welcome," shouts the valiant Hob, " here I'll stand, I'll take no other than St. George's guard ; if he lets drive at me, fore Gad, I'll hit 'en over the sconce, if he was a Knight of Gould."

Sure enough, he does crack Old Testie's crown, and Sir Thomas has to draw his sword and beat him and his comrades off, not without bloodshed.

Friendly at once seizes the opportunity to get the ladies down from the balcony, where they had been so safely guarded hitherto, and goes off with Flora, while Woodvill walks away with Lucia, but returns to meet Lady Testie, who disappears in turn with him.

Sir Thomas, having been a trifle hasty with his sword, is meanwhile arrested by the Constable and the Watch ; but the Surgeon assures Friendly that Hob's head was far too thick to be damaged seriously, though he has been almost terrified to death, and the fifth act begins with a ludicrous scene in which Hob (imagining himself mortally wounded) bequeaths all his worldly goods (including his 'bacca-box and his new leather breeches) to his sweetheart Mary. Surgeon Probe, however, advises meat and drink, and after a hearty meal good Hob announces himself as " fine and spract now."

Sir Thomas, in prison and supposing himself likely to be hanged for murder, is visited by his daughter, who pretends to be under the same delusion, and so commends herself by her grief that he forgives her disobedience and hands her a deed of gift of half his estate. She then turns to Friendly who has been present in the disguise of a lawyer, and the two are about to be united at last, when Woodvill interposes, under the impression that Flora was the lady who had been so kind to him the night before. The two friends are about to quarrel, when Lady Testie, masked, comes in and quietly convinces Woodvill of his error. She then goes out again, and returns, unmasked, to tell Sir Thomas that he will be released, as Hob is after all in no danger of death. This tidings she conveys to her husband with so good a grace that he pardons both young men (whose disguise he had at first been angry enough to discover) and gives Flora to Friendly and Lucia to Woodvill, who is consoled by Lady Testie's generosity for her now inevitable fidelity to the amorous Sir Thomas. The play ends with the entrance of Hob, who announces he is ready to marry his Mary on the spot.

Leguerre's engravings show two other scenes in which Hob is apparently thrown down a well by the enraged Sir Thomas, and rescued by his father and mother ; but these do not occur in the version of the play kindly lent me by Mr. Broadley, and I suspect that they were only inserted in the ballad-farce called *Flora, or Hob-in-the-Well*, which Cibber founded upon Doggett's original. The Epilogue and Prologue are of course an integral part of the original text, which was acted by royal command before King George I in April, 1717, on the boards of Drury Lane. But the verses sung by various characters during the progress of the play only occur in Leguerre's engravings and were interpolated in the later edition by Cibber.

APPENDIX II

FISHMONGERS' HALL, LONDON
DOGGETT'S COAT AND BADGE WAGER
LONDON BRIDGE TO CHELSEA

WATERMEN who are, or will be, out of their time on or before Tuesday, the 9th July, 1901, and who may be entitled to compete for the above Wager, will be permitted to take up their Freedom at a Court which will be held on that day, and those who are out of their time on the 14th July will be permitted to take up their Freedom at a Special Court which will be held for that purpose on Monday, the 15th July, provided that previous notice be given to the Clerk to the Watermen's Company.

THE FISHMONGERS' COMPANY, in order to the selection of the best men to row for the Wager, direct the men who intend to row to give in their names at the Watermen's Hall, not later than 4'clock on Monday, the 15th July, and attend that evening at 6 o'clock at Fishmongers' Hall, London Bridge, to have their names registered, and to pay a deposit of Ten Shillings each, such deposit will be forfeited in the event of a Competitor not rowing the entire distance either in the Trial Heats or Wager. Should it be necessary to have Trial Heats, they will be rowed on Tuesday, the 16th July.

Prior to rowing the Trial Heats, Candidates will be balloted for to ascertain in which heat and position each accepted Candidate is to row.

If there be more than Six Heats, the first man in each, shall, unless otherwise settled, row the course again, to determine the six men who are to row the Wager on Thursday, the 1st August, from London Bridge to Chelsea.

No Cutter or other Boat will, under any circumstances, be permitted to accompany any of the Competitors. Any contravention of this order will disqualify the offending Competitor.

The Course for the Trial Heats will be from Putney Bridge to Hammersmith Bridge, or the reverse.

The Trial Heats and the Wager will be rowed under the direction of the Company's Bargemaster.

The following sums will be allowed in the Trial Heats, viz. :

							£		
To the 1st man in each Heat	..	.	.	.	.	.	£1	1	0
,, 2nd ,, ,,	.	.	.	.	.	.	0	15	0
,, 3rd ,, ,,	.	.	.	.	.	.	0	10	0
And to each of the other men, provided he rows the distance							0	7	6

Five Shillings will be allowed to each man for the hire of a Wager Boat on the Trial Heat.

The Prizes to be given to the Competitors on the 1st August will be:

To the Winner of the Coat and Badge		.	.	.	.	£10	0	0
,,	Second man	{including Jolliffe's Gift}	.	.	.	6	0	0
,,	Third	,,		.	.	.	5	0	0
,,	Fourth	,,	.	.	.	.	.	.	.	4	0	0
,,	Fifth	,,	.	.	.	.	.	.	.	3	0	0
,,	Sixth	,,	.	.	.	.	.	.	.	2	0	0

provided they row the entire distance, and subject to the usual conditions.

J. WRENCH TOWSE,
Clerk to the Fishmongers' Company.

June, 1901.

APPENDIX III

DOGGETT'S COAT AND BADGE.

FISHMONGERS' HALL.

THE Names of the Six Young Watermen who are to row on Friday, the 3rd August, 1906, for the Livery and Badge, given by Mr. THOMAS DOGGETT, deceased, a famous Comedian, in commemoration of the happy Acenssion of the Family of His present Majesty to the Throne of Great Britain, are :—

Station.

Cobb, Henry Robert	.	.	.	(Blue) Putney.
Carder, Percy John	.	.	.	(Green) Christchurch.
Fell, Thomas	.	.	.	(Yellow) Chiswick.
Bushnell, John Henry	.	.	.	(White) Richmond.
Dyckhoff, Harold Rechab	.	.	.	(Pink) Erith.
Brewer, Edwin Lewis	.	.	.	(Red) Putney.

The Prizes are—provided they row the entire distance, and subject to the conditions of the Wager being strictly complied with :—

To the 1st man, £10 0 0 by the Company, in addition to the Coat and Badge under Mr. DOGGETT's Will.

    „   2nd   „   6 0 0 ⎰ Including Sir William Joliffe's Gift of
    „   3rd   „   5 0 0 ⎱ £7 3s. 4d.

    „   4th   „   4 0 0 ⎫
    „   5th   „   3 0 0 ⎬ The Company's Gifts.
    „   6th   „   2 0 0 ⎭

The Competitors will start from London Bridge shortly after 12 o'clock noon to row to Chelsea.

July, 1906.

APPENDIX IV

The occupation of Thames Watermen is very different now, as we have seen, from what it was in the sixteenth century; and even in the present generation a slow but constant change is still in progress. As an interesting example of these developments I therefore append an article on the " Gravesend Watermen " which appeared in the *Daily Telegraph* for April 28, 1908 :—

Decidedly a picturesque figure is the Gravesend waterman. To see him lolling on the pier, too, one might suppose that his occupation was unassailable, and that all the while the tides continue to ebb and flow the river is sure to afford him a comfortable livelihood. But, as a matter of fact, the waterman is just now in anything but a contented frame of mind. The passing of the sailing ship has largely contributed to his undoing, and so little does he think of future prospects that he and his fellows have lately formed an organization of their own to protect what is left of their means of living. These expert boat-handlers have a recollection that gradually grows more dim of the days when they reaped a golden harvest. That was when full-rigged clipper ships carried cabins full of passengers to or from our most distant possessions. Homeward bound from India or Australia, or outward bound for those far countries, the ships of a former age always dropped anchor off Gravesend. There were passengers to be taken aboard or ashore, there was much business to be done on the ship's account, and the Gravesend boatmen pursued what might almost be called a princely occupation.

Sail and Steam.

To-day the sailing ships traversing the Thames are few and far between, and hardly any of them carry passengers. The sharp-stemmed liner has taken their place, and her passengers are more or less independent of the waterman. Should there happen to be a large number of people to be taken off, it is not the waterman who gets the job, but a ferry-boat, which comes alongside and does the work rapidly and on a large scale. The modern waterman has sense enough to understand that the use of a steamboat in these circumstances is inevitable. But he does not like it, all the same. More particularly does he argue that where only a few passengers have to be landed the row-boat ought still to be employed. But it would be unfair to give the impression that the Gravesend waterman is merely competent to take a passenger ashore, or to row him out to a ship. He has not served a seven-years' apprenticeship merely in order to qualify himself to do that. The truth is these watermen are experts in all matters appertaining to the River Thames. As river pilots their knowledge is as thorough as it well could be, while in warping a ship into or out of dock, or in making her fast to mooring buoys in the stream, they display extraordinary skill.

Handling of Boats.

Nevertheless, it may be said that it is in the handling of open boats in a tidal river that the Gravesend watermen particularly excel. Probably there are no better river boatmen to be found in any port of the world. For the most part the handling of boats under sail and under oars is a neglected art. The late Stuart Moore, who was an authority in these matters, had the highest possible opinion of Gravesend watermen's skill in this direction. Indeed, not very long before his death, he urged the Admiralty to put its pride in its pocket, and to engage Gravesend watermen to teach young officers of the Navy how to work tides and judge of their effect, how to board a vessel, how to touch at a pier or a wharf, how to take a tow, and how to bring up to a mooring. The training of the nerve, the judging of the forces of wind and sea under varying conditions, the estimating of distances between moving objects— these are things to be learned when you are young, and it is the young waterman who picks them up to perfection. Whether eventually the Gravesend watermen will find their occupation in giving instructions to midshipmen is problematical, but the mere fact that such a proposal was put forward by so competent an authority as Mr. Stuart Moore is perhaps the best proof that this race of experts is worth preserving.

Taking a Tow

To commend the Gravesend watermen for their ability to take a tow is to praise an art which the landsman will hardly understand. It is one that needs great skill. A big steamer is coming up the Thames. She is light, and her sides tower high above the water. Near by are watermen in what, by comparison, is a cockleshell. It seems almost impossible that the small boat can be taken in tow without the aid of the steamer, or, at least, without the cognisance of those on board. But the Gravesend waterman is an adept at hooking on while the steamer maintains her speed. Lying on the thwarts of the watermen's boat is a long, stout pole, with, at one end of it, a powerful iron hook, with wide jaws. Made fast to the other end of the pole is a long coil of rope. The boat is down the river below Gravesend, and badly wants a tow up stream, because wind and tide are against her in her efforts to get back home. Perhaps the waterman and his mate have been in attendance in Higham Bight on a vessel which has come home from the Colonies, and have undertaken to land one or two of the ship's company. The boat is pulled out into the fairway, until she almost seems in danger of being run down by a big cargo steamer which is punting along at, say, nine knots. " That'll do for us," says the boatman to his mate, and the latter gets his hook ready.

Hooking On.

The boat is kept just ahead of the place where the steamer will pass. To the novice it is a thrilling moment, for it seems almost certain that the little craft will be sent to the bottom. But those in charge of her know their work. At the last moment she is brought close under the steamer's bow, and when this is level with the row-boat, the waterman's mate is seen standing forward with the hooked pole. When about half the steamer's length has passed, the row-boat meantime getting plenty of motion from the wash, the man with the hook deftly places it over the steamer's bulwarks. As the steamer forges ahead, the iron hook grates along the rail, and, perhaps, falls overboard. That, of course, means that the attempt to hook on has failed, and that there is nothing for it but to wait for another upcoming steamer. This time the operation is attended with success. The hooked pole holds, and then comes another exciting moment. The steamer runs off with the pole, the boatman rapidly pays out the rope made fast to the end of it, and all the time the little boat is wallowing about in the most disagreeable fashion. Presently, when it is thought that a sufficient scope of rope has been run out, the boatman catches a turn round the forward thwart. At once the rope tautens, and with a forward jump the row-boat is hauled through the water at a swishing pace. Her bow rises, and her stern sinks, and she throws up a fine spray which flies all over the occupants of the boat.

Very like a Whale.

In this way the boat is towed along by the side of the steamer, and a long way forward of her propeller. The rudder, of course, is deftly used to keep the boat away from the ship's side. The sensation when the row-boat first shoots ahead is a shock such as a whaler's boat's crew experience when they make fast to the leviathan of the deep. Nobody on board the steamer pays any attention to the boat, for it is a recognized practice for watermen to steal a tow in this fashion. The hook may score the paint on the ship's rail, but that does not matter, for it is all in the day's work. Sometimes, but not often, those on board the steamer are disinclined to let go the towing-hook when the watermen want to be cast off. In such a case, when a vessel is outward bound, there would appear to be nothing for it but for the boatmen to proceed to sea with the vessel, or cut the rope and lose the pole.

Casting Off.

But the Gravesend men are quite equal to an emergency. In such a case the boat is brought as near as is permissible to the ship's side, and one of the men climbs up the pole, carrying with him a rope, of which one end is already made fast to the boat. Having clambered up the pole and reached the rail, he passes the rope round a stanchion and throws the end to his mate in the boat, who makes it fast. In this way he has provided himself with a means of return. Having cast off the hook, he slides down the ropes into the boat. One end of the hawser is at once let go, runs round the stanchion, and falls into the water. The boat is then clear, and in a few seconds is well astern of the steamer's propeller, which is busily churning up spray that turns into rainbows. It is monkeys' work this, but it is a task of which the Gravesend waterman thinks nothing. But it indicates the sort of stuff of which he is made, and at least suggests that if his occupation should unhappily disappear a set of brave and resourceful men will be driven from the bosom of the Thames.

TIGER OF THE STRIPE